The Meters of Greek and Latin Poetry

Revised Edition

by

James W. Halporn

Martin Ostwald

and

Thomas G. Rosenmeyer

Hackett Publishing Company, Inc.

Indianapolis/Cambridge

Copyright © 1963 by James Halporn, Martin Ostwald, and
    Thomas Rosenmeyer (published: Methuen, London, 1963;
    Bobbs-Merrill, Indianapolis and New York, 1963).
    Assigned 1979 to University of Oklahoma Press.
Revised edition copyright © 1980 by
    University of Oklahoma Press, Norman
Reprinted with permission 1994 by
    Hackett Publishing Company, Inc.

Printed in the United States of America

For further information, please address
    Hackett Publishing Company, Inc., Box 44937
    Indianapolis, Indiana 46244-0937

Library of Congress Cataloging-in-Publication Data

Halporn, James W.
    The meters of Greek and Latin poetry / by James W. Halporn,
Martin Ostwald, and Thomas G. Rosenmeyer. — Rev. ed.
        p.   cm.
    Originally published: Norman : University of Oklahoma Press,
c. 1980.
    Includes bibliographical references and index.
    ISBN 0-87220-244-5. — ISBN 0-87220-243-7 (pbk.)
        1. Classical languages—Metrics and rhythmics.   I. Ostwald,
Martin, 1922-   . II. Rosenmeyer, Thomas G.   III. Title.
PA186.H25   1994
881'.0109—dc20   93-47104
                                                                CIP

The paper used in this publication meets the minimum requirements
of American National Standard for Information Sciences—Permanence
of Paper for Printed Library Materials, ANSI Z39.48-1984.

∞

Contents

iv

Preface

The purpose of this book is not to make a new contribution to metrical theory, but to present the English-speaking student with as clear and simple an outline of Greek and Latin meters as he needs in order to read the verse of the Greeks and Romans as poetry. In metrics, perhaps more than in most other fields of classical scholarship, a new book has to rely heavily upon its predecessors, and the present work is no exception.

The modern study of metrics can be said to begin with the work of U. von Wilamowitz-Moellendorff and of Paul Maas. Building upon and expanding their results, Bruno Snell published his lucid and penetrating *Griechische Metrik*[3] (Göttingen 1962), and we are indebted to him for permitting us to use his arrangement in presenting the complexities of classical meters and to draw freely on the content of his work. In addition, the following works have been most frequently consulted in the preparation of this book, and, like Snell's *Griechische Metrik*, they are recommended to the student for additional information and discussion: A. M. Dale, *The Lyric Metres of Greek Drama* (Cambridge 1948); K. Rupprecht, *Einführung in die griechische Metrik*[3] (München 1950); W. J. W. Koster, *Traité de métrique grecque suivi d'un précis de métrique latine*[2] (Leyden 1953); F. Crusius, *Römische Metrik*, 4th ed. by H. Rubenbauer (München 1959); and L. Nougaret, *Traité de métrique latine classique*[2] (Paris 1956). For the metrics of Alcman, Sappho and Alcaeus, and Corinna, see also the excellent commentaries of D. L. Page in his special Oxford editions.

Wherever feasible, we have used the same arrangement of

v

the various sections in both the Greek and the Latin parts, in order to facilitate the use of one part in conjunction with the other. The two parts are, nevertheless, conceived as essentially independent of one another and, as a result, some of the material found in the Latin part is merely a repetition – sometimes verbatim – or adaptation of what is stated in the Greek part. But while in the Latin part the symbols for long and short syllables are placed above each line, it was found more convenient to place them below the line in Greek quotations in order not to interfere with accents and breathings.

The quotations from the classical texts are from the following editions: B. Snell, ed., *Pindarus*² (Teubner 1955); B. Snell, ed., *Bacchylides*⁷ (Teubner 1958); E. Lobel and D. Page, edd., *Poetarum Lesbiorum Fragmenta* (Oxford 1955); E. Diehl, ed., *Anthologia Lyrica Graeca*, 2nd and 3rd edd. (Teubner 1924, 1936, 1949, 1950, 1952); F. Klingner, ed., *Horatius*³ (Teubner 1959). All other authors are cited from the editions in the *Oxford Classical Texts*; where an author is not available in that series, the reference is to the Teubner edition. When other editions had to be used, the name of the editor or the publication is appended.

The preparation of the Greek part was undertaken by Professor T. G. Rosenmeyer, largely on the model of Snell's *Griechische Metrik*; in the Latin part, sections I–VIII and XX are the work of Professor J. W. Halporn and sections IX–XIX of Professor M. Ostwald. Although each author is ultimately responsible only for his own contribution, we greatly profited from each other's criticisms and from the criticisms and suggestions of many kind friends and colleagues, foremost among them Miss A. M. Dale.

JAMES W. HALPORN

MARTIN OSTWALD

THOMAS G. ROSENMEYER

The Meters of Greek Poetry

The Meters of Greek Poetry

1. Sigla

— longum, i.e., a long element in the scheme = space for one long syllable

◡ breve, i.e., a short element in the scheme = space for one short syllable

× anceps, i.e., space for one long or one short syllable

∧ lack of one element:

> 1. *acephaly* ("headlessness") at the beginning of the Aeolic base (cf. below, section 16)
> 2. *catalexis* (suppression of the final element) at the end of a period (cf. below, section 3.4)

/ regular occurrence of break, i.e., word ending (cf. below, section 4)

/ / alternative positions of break (cf. below, section 5)

// pause, i.e., end of period (cf. below, section 3)

/// end of strophe (cf. below, section 9)

⌒ bridge, i.e., word ending between the two elements avoided or not permitted (cf. below, section 4)

ia iamb: × — ◡ — *

tro trochee: — ◡ — ×

cr cretic: — ◡ —

ba bacchiac: ◡ — —   ⎱ Iambo-trochaic meters; see

lec lecythion: — ◡ — × — ◡ —   ⎰ below, section 12

ith ithyphallic: — ◡ — ◡ — —

---

* Notation and sigla represent one metron, i.e., one minimal or standard unit of the meter in question.

3

da	dactyl: $-\overset{\cup}{\smile}\overset{\cup}{\smile}$ *	
an	anapaest: $\overset{\cup}{\smile}\overset{\cup}{\smile}\,\overset{\cup\cup}{}\,\overset{\cup}{\smile}\overset{\cup}{\smile}\,\overset{\cup\cup}{}$	
io	ionic: $\cup\,\cup--$	⎱
cho	choriamb: $-\cup\cup-$	Ionic meters; see below,
anacl	anaclast: $\cup\cup-\cup-\underset{.}{\cup}--$	⎰ section 13
doch	dochmiac: $\times--\cup-$ †	
gl	glyconic: $\times\times-\cup\cup-\cup-$	⎱ Aeolic meters; see
ph	pherecratean: $\times\times-\cup\cup--$	below, section
hipp	hipponactean: $\times\times-\cup\cup-\cup--$	⎰ 16
D	$-\cup\cup-\cup\cup-$	⎱
d^1	$-\cup\cup-$	
d^2	$\cup\cup-$	Dactylo-epitritic meter; see below,
E	$-\cup-\times-\cup-$	section 17. 2
e	$-\cup-$	⎰

2. Metrics and Prosody

The rhythm of classical Greek poetry is determined by the "flow" (Greek: ῥυθμός) or succession of long and short elements. Unlike English poetry whose rhythm is largely the result of the arrangement of stressed and unstressed syllables, Greek verse is measured by predominantly quantitative standards. Down to the end of the fifth century B.C. and beyond, most poetry exhibits certain identifiable metrical patterns; long elements and short elements are distributed according to traditional rules which allow us to divide the mass of poetic forms into a number of characteristic genres or meters.‡

* In case of alternatives, the more common quantities are printed level, the less common quantities above them.

† This is the basic form of the dochmiac, of which there are many variations; see below, section 19.

‡ In this survey the terms *ictus*, *arsis*, and *thesis* will not be used; they might easily create the false impression that Greek verse operated significantly with a stress accent, or that it was measured by a regular musical "beat". Cf. also the *Glossary of Technical Terms*.

4

By a long element we understand the space in the metric scheme where a long syllable is expected; by a short element we understand the space where a short syllable is expected; and by an anceps we understand the space where either a long or a short syllable may be expected.

A long syllable is a syllable whose vowel is naturally long ($\bar{a}$, η, $\bar{\iota}$, $\bar{v}$, ω, $a\iota$, $\epsilon\iota$, $\eta\iota$, $o\iota$, $v\iota$, $\omega\iota$, av, ϵv, ov) or a closed syllable, i.e., a syllable terminating in a consonant. All other syllables are short. For example, in $\lambda\breve{\iota}-\pi os$ the first syllable is short, in $\gamma\rho\bar{\iota}-\phi os$ and $\breve{\iota}\pi-\pi os$ it is long; so it is in $\pi\breve{v}\xi os = \pi\breve{v}\kappa-\sigma os$. A single consonant separating two syllables or two words is felt to introduce the second rather than terminate the first syllable; thus, in the phrase $\kappa a\lambda\grave{o}\nu$ $\mathring{a}\nu\delta\rho a$, the final syllable of $\kappa a\lambda\acute{o}\nu$ is treated as an open syllable: κa-λo-$\nu a\nu$-$\delta\rho a$. The first syllable of a word like $\pi\acute{\epsilon}\tau\rho os$ is counted either short or long; the treatment of the combination of a mute (γ, β, δ, κ, π, τ, χ, ϕ, θ) with a liquid (λ, ρ, more rarely μ, ν) varies depending on whether the mute is felt to close the preceding syllable ($\pi\epsilon\tau$-ρos) or, in association with the liquid, to begin the next syllable ($\pi\epsilon$-$\tau\rho os$).

Example: Sophocles, *Philoctetes* 296:

$$\mathring{a}\lambda\lambda' \ \mathring{\epsilon}\nu \ \pi\acute{\epsilon}\tau\rho o\iota\sigma\iota \ \pi\acute{\epsilon}\tau\rho o\nu \ \mathring{\epsilon}\kappa\tau\rho\acute{\iota}\beta\omega\nu \ \mu\acute{o}\lambda\iota s$$

Here the treatment of mute plus liquid in the same word differs within one line. Some authors allow themselves more variety in this regard than others. In the Aeolic lyrics of Sappho and Alcaeus, the syllable preceding the mute is *always* counted long; in the Homeric epic it is *usually* counted long, and sometimes short; while in Attic tragedy there is no distinct preference for either long or short.

Occasionally two adjoining vowels are treated, and probably pronounced, as if they were one. When the vowels occur within the same word, the process is called *synizesis*.

5

Example: Iliad 1. 1.:

$$\Pi\eta\lambda\eta\ddot{\imath}\acute{a}\delta\epsilon\omega$$

When the vowels are separated by a word ending, the process is called *synaloephe.*

Example: Sophocles, *Philoctetes* 1202:

$$\H{a}\rho\theta\rho o\nu\ \H{a}\pi\hat{\omega}\sigma a\iota.\ \H{a}\lambda\lambda'$$

It might be mentioned here that the analysis and interpretation of new papyrus finds is greatly assisted by our increasing knowledge of the special practices of the various writers in matters of prosody. But we must be careful not to regard those practices as rigid rules. To cite just one example, in fr. 44 LP, a poem in which Sappho is dealing with an epic theme, she allows short final syllable before mute plus liquid, and even permits epic correption (cf. below, section 5) which is not used in standard Aeolic poetry. This should warn us that the archaic poets, like the Hellenistic writers at a later time, could vary their metrical and prosodic techniques to achieve a variety of aesthetic effects.

3. The Period

Greek verses are divided by means of *pauses* (siglum: //). These pauses, distinguishing one metrical sequence from the next, are marked by one or more of the following:

1. *Word ending.* This is mandatory; a pause is an emphatic break. Note that in metrics a word cluster equals a word. Enclitics and postpositives such as γὰρ or μέν join with the preceding word to form one word cluster; prepositives such as σύν and καί and the article join with the following word to form one word cluster. A break or pause rarely occurs between the units of such a word cluster.

2. *hiatus*, i.e., the gap between a word ending in a vowel and a word beginning with a vowel.

Example: Sophocles, *Philoctetes* 641–2:

ὅταν φεύγῃς κακά. ‖ οὔκ, ἀλλὰ

Hiatus is avoided in most types of Greek verse, unless it occurs in the position of an emphatic break. But contrast the practice of the epic hexameter (cf. below, section 5 with note on p. 12).*

3. *brevis in longo*, i.e., the use of a short syllable in the last element, despite the general rule that the last element is always counted long metrically.

Example: Sophocles, *Philoctetes* 647:

καίπερ οὐ πολλῶν ἄπο.
‿ ‖

Thus a short syllable is often found in the final element of the dactylic hexameter where it is then counted long (cf. below, section 5 with note on p. 10).

Example: Odyssey 1. 1:

ὃς μάλα πολλὰ‖

4. *catalexis*, i.e., "coming to an abrupt end" (siglum: . . . ‿). This term is used to describe the suppression of the final element of a meter before a pause; a preceding short element is then automatically lengthened. Catalexis is particularly common at the end of a strophe (cf. below, section 9). For an example see below, section 8.

The metrical units thus separated by pauses are called *periods*. They are the basic units, and any analysis of metrical

---

* Hiatus is often, especially in Epic and Attic poetry, avoided by *elision*, the elimination of a final short vowel, or *aphaeresis*, the elimination of an initial short vowel.

7

patterns must start with them. In spoken verse, line and period are usually identical; that is to say, each line of the printed text terminates in a pause. In lyric verse the period is often longer than the line of the printed text.

Example: Aeschylus, *Suppliants* 17–18:

$$\beta o \grave{o} s \ \grave{\epsilon} \xi \ \grave{\epsilon} \pi a \phi \widehat{\eta} s \ \kappa \grave{a} \xi \ \grave{\epsilon} \pi \iota \pi \nu o \acute{\iota} a s$$
$$\cup\cup \ - \ \cup\cup \ - \ / \ - \ \cup\cup \ - \ - \ /$$

$$\varDelta \iota \grave{o} s \ \epsilon \mathring{v} \chi \acute{o} \mu \epsilon \nu o \nu \ \tau \epsilon \tau \acute{\epsilon} \lambda \epsilon \sigma \tau a \iota .$$
$$\cup\cup \ - \ \cup \ \cup - / \cup \ \cup - - \ //$$

The punctuation, which marks an emphatic break, and the catalectic ending – line 18 has one syllable less at the end than line 17 – indicate that line 18 terminates in a pause, i.e., completes a period. The lack of an emphatic break or catalexis at the end of line 17 and the unbroken carry-over of the rhythm from line 17 to line 18 suggest that lines 17 and 18 together form one period, or part of one period. In strophic compositions (cf. below, section 9) a pause usually cannot be safely identified until both strophe and antistrophe or several repeated systems have been checked (cf. below, section 17. 1).

4. Caesura, Diaeresis, Bridge

The rhythm of poetry is determined not only by the distribution of longa and brevia but also by the fact that in certain positions word ending is either forbidden (or avoided) or mandatory (or recommended). The avoidance of a word ending in a certain position in a meter is called *bridge* * (siglum: ⌢. The siglum ⌢ refers only to the elements directly below it; hence ⌣͡ means that the bridge goes into operation only when the first element is long). The place where a word ending is expected is called *caesura* if the break occurs *within* the limits of a metron, and *diaeresis* if the break occurs *be-*

---

* The Greek term *zeugma* is not used in this survey in order to avoid confusion with *zeugma* in the grammatical sense.

tween two metra. In this survey, caesura and diaeresis are noted by the same siglum: /.

It is often easier to note the presence of a bridge than to register the range of possible breaks.* For most meters, indeed, the natural articulation of the verse by means of breaks has not yet been fully studied.

The most famous bridge is that discovered by Richard Porson (in his 1802 edition of Euripides' *Hecuba*) for the end of the tragic iambic trimeter (cf. below, section 7), namely: the anceps of the third metron cannot be occupied by a long syllable terminating a word: . . . . $\widehat{\cup}- \cup - //$. Similar bridges have been detected in the trochaic tetrameter (cf. below, section 8), in the early Dactylo-epitrites (cf. below, section 17. 2), and in some other lyric meters.

Conversely, caesurae and diaereses occur in many positions.

Example of a common caesura: Sophocles, *Philoctetes* 664:

μόνος δέδωκας, ὃς χθόν' Οἰταίαν ἰδεῖν
∪— ∪ — ∪ / — ˘∪ — — — ∪— //

where the break falls within an iambic metron (cf. below, section 7).

Example of an equally common diaeresis: Sophocles, *Ajax* 134:

Τελαμώνιε παῖ, τῆς ἀμφιρύτου
∪∪— ∪∪ — / — — ∪∪— //

where the break falls between two anapaestic metra (cf. below, section 11). Most periods exhibit more than one characteristic break (caesura or diaeresis) each, as is apparent in the structure of the hexameter (cf. below, section 5).

---

* A bridge is a non-break; a break is a non-bridge. But the inverse correspondence is not complete. In a given piece of choral lyric, for instance, a particular bridge may be observed throughout the strophic repetitions, while a particular break occurs only in a majority of them. In fact there seems to be some evidence to suggest that a bridge impinged more sharply on the aesthetic awareness of the listener than a break.

9

Another important factor in determining the rhythm of Greek poetry is the relationship between the length of a word and its position in the verse. Monosyllabic words, for instance, are favored only in certain positions in the period; in some meters they may not appear immediately before or after certain breaks. This is an important aspect of the study of metrics, but since many of its findings are still subject to scholarly controversy the present survey will not touch on them.

5. The Hexameter

The Homeric hexameter (6 da$_\wedge$//) * is the oldest known Greek meter. Later hexameters, such as those of Callimachus and Nonnus, differ from the Homeric only in allowing less variety in the use of caesura and the substitution of longum for double breve.

In the epic hexameter, two brevia can always be replaced by one longum, but not vice versa. Hence we may speak of trisyllabic ($-\cup\cup$) and dissyllabic ($--$) dactyls. The final dactyl is always dissyllabic, with *brevis in longo* permitted because each hexameter constitutes one period (cf. above, section 3. 3). The fifth dactyl is usually trisyllabic; an exception occurs especially when a heavy word, occupying a metron and a half or more, is used at the end of the period.

Example: Iliad 1. 14:

$$\underset{\cup-\ \cup\ \cup\ --\ --\ -//}{\text{ἐκηβόλου Ἀπόλλωνος}}$$

The most prominent caesurae are those found after the third longum,

---

* Strictly speaking the hexameter is not catalectic, since it ends in a full dissyllabic dactyl. But in order to distinguish this ending from the lyric dactylic clausula $-\cup-$ (cf. below, section 10. 3 (b)), it is more convenient to describe the hexameter as a catalectic meter.

Example: Iliad 1. 1.:

Μῆνιν ἄειδε θεά, Πηληϊάδεω 'Αχιλῆος
‒ ∪ ∪‒∪ ∪‒/ ‒ ‒∪∪‒ ∪∪‒ ‒//

and after the first short element of the third metron,

Example: Odyssey 1. 1:

"Ανδρα μοι ἔννεπε, Μοῦσα, πολύτροπον, ὃς μάλα πολλὰ
‒ ∪ ∪ ‒∪∪ ‒ ∪/∪‒ ∪∪ ‒ ∪∪ ‒ ‒//

or, less frequently, after the fourth longum.

Example: Iliad 1. 145:

ἢ Αἴας ἢ 'Ιδομενεὺς ἢ δῖος 'Οδυσσεὺς
‒ ‒ ‒ ‒ ∪∪ ‒/ ‒ ‒∪ ∪‒ ‒//

Note that the tendency is to avoid dividing the line precisely in the middle (diaeresis after the third dactyl), which would break up the unity of the period. A break after the first short element of the fourth metron is very rare (cf. Bridges, above, p. 9).

Example: Iliad 9. 394 (as read in the manuscripts):

Πηλεύς θήν μοι ἔπειτα γυναῖκα γαμέσσεται αὐτός.
‒ ‒ ‒ ∪ ∪‒∪∪ ‒ ∪/∪‒ ∪∪ ‒ ‒//

Diaeresis after a trisyllabic fourth metron (cf. *Odyssey* 1. 1, cited above) is often called *bucolic* because it is characteristic of the pastoral poetry of the Alexandrians, which avoids diaeresis after dissyllabic fourth metron (for this avoidance, cf. also the hexameters of Archilochus, Solon, and Theognis).

Example: Theocritus *Idyll* 1. 1–13; note that in half of these lines the "bucolic diaeresis" is marked by punctuation. In his non-pastoral poems Theocritus does not employ this form of the hexameter with the same frequency; see, for instance, *Idyll* 15.

If we count word clusters as outlined above, section 3.1, the hexameter usually breaks into four parts, as follows: *

‒/∪/∪/‒/∪ ‒/∪/∪/‒/∪ ∪/‒ ∪ ∪‒‒//
A¹A²A³A⁴   B¹B²   C¹   C²

* The scheme is that of H. Fraenkel, *Wege und Formen*² (Munich 1960) 104, who notes the breaks rather than the bridges. The three breaks are given as Λ, B, and C.

Note that there are fewer breaks, and that the choice of breaks becomes less varied, as we proceed towards the end of the period. *Heavy* words may disturb the regularity of the scheme.

Examples: Iliad 1. 1, cited above, where the third break (C) is shifted forward, and *Iliad* 1. 145, cited above, where the second break (B) is eliminated altogether.

In epic hexameters, hiatus between words is more common than in other meters. Where hiatus occurs, a long final vowel or diphthong is often shortened metrically. This is called *epic correption.*

Example: Iliad 1. 29:

$$\underset{\smile\ \ -}{\tau\grave{\eta}\nu\ \delta'\ \grave{\epsilon}\gamma\grave{\omega}\ o\grave{\upsilon}\ \lambda\acute{\upsilon}\sigma\omega}\cdot{}^{*}$$

6. The Elegiac Couplet

In the elegiac couplet, a hexameter is combined into one scheme with a second line which consists of a duplication of the *hemiepes* ("half-verse"), i.e., the part of the hexameter before the caesura after the third longum (a blunt dactylic trimeter; cf. below, section 10. 3): $-\smile\smile-\smile\smile-$ (notation: 3 da$_{\wedge\wedge}$). The two hemiepes are always separated by diaeresis. Like the hexameter, this second line, in spite of its double nature, consists of only one period. Its usual form is as follows:

$$-\,\overset{\frown}{\smile\smile}-\overset{\frown}{\smile\smile}-/-\smile\smile-\smile\smile-//\qquad 3\ \text{da}_{\wedge\wedge}/3\ \text{da}_{\wedge\wedge}//$$

* Uncorrepted hiatus may often be explained as caused by an old initial digamma which has dropped out in the writing. But it is generally agreed that the epic hexameter is not always fashioned with the most rigorous attention to the rules of prosody. Long syllables are sometimes read as short *(example: Iliad* 16. 857: ἀνδροτῆτα), and short syllables are read as long *(examples: Iliad* 4. 155: φίλε and 11. 36: βλοσυρῶπις ἐστεφάνωτο). For further details, see K. Meister, *Homerische Kunstsprache* (1921), pp. 34 ff.

Example: Solon fr. 1 D. 1–2:

Μνημοσύνης καὶ Ζηνὸς Ὀλυμπίου ἀγλαὰ τέκνα,
— ‿ ‿ — — — ‿ / ‿ — ‿‿ — ‿‿ — — //

Μοῦσαι Πιερίδες, κλῦτέ μοι εὐχομένῳ·
— — — ‿‿ — / — ‿ ‿ — ‿‿ — ///

More often than not, as in the example cited, the first line of
an elegiac couplet has caesura after the first short element of
the third metron rather than after the third longum, though
the latter is almost as common. The purpose seems to be to
avoid a steady coincidence between the caesura of the hexa-
meter and the diaeresis of the second line.

The elegiac couplet came to be used particularly for short
funerary *epigrams*, often consisting of as few as one or two
couplets, or for longer poems usually of a reflective or semi-
philosophical nature. A poem of the latter type is called an
elegy; example: Solon fr. 1 D., the beginning of which is cited
above. Many of the funerary epigrams are attributed to
Simonides; for an epigram which may be by Archilochus,
see below, *Appendix*, pp. 54–55. Beginning with the Hellen-
istic writers the epigram was used for many purposes where
succinctness and pungency was desired, though it continued
to be used also for funerary inscriptions.

7. *The Iambic Trimeter*

The basic structure of the trimeter is as follows:

$$\times - \cup - \times \overset{/}{|} - \cup \overset{/}{|} - \overset{\frown}{\cup} - \cup - \; // \qquad 3 \text{ ia } //$$

Note Porson's bridge (see above, section 4). The chief caesura
is more commonly found after the second anceps than after
the second breve. Thus, as in the case of the dactylic hexa-
meter, the second half of the verse is usually longer than the
first. In tragic verse, a break in the middle of the line, i.e.,
after the first longum of the second metron is rare. Ex-
ample: Eur. *Suppl.* 1, where an elision mitigates the effect.

According to Aristotle, *Poetics* 4. 14. 1449a 24–26 the iambic trimeter is of all meters the closest approximation to ordinary speech. Hence it was used in contexts where poetic elevation or embellishment was not a desideratum, as in the conversational passages of Attic drama.

The older iambic poets (iambographers), the three tragedians, and Aristophanes differ greatly in their handling of the trimeter. Generally speaking, the older writers deviate least from the basic structure, whereas comedy permits itself a great deal of freedom. Bridges and breaks, for instance, are less closely observed in comedy than in tragedy. Perhaps the most striking difference between comic and tragic dialogue is the greater frequency and range of *resolution*. That is, in comedy two shorts may be substituted freely for a longum, an anceps, or even a short element.

Example: Aristophanes, *Clouds* 21 :

$$\phi\acute{\epsilon}\rho' \ \ddot{\iota}\delta\omega \ \tau\acute{\iota} \ \grave{o}\phi\epsilon\acute{\iota}\lambda\omega; \ \delta\acute{\omega}\delta\epsilon\kappa\alpha \ \mu\nu\hat{\alpha}\varsigma \ \Pi\alpha\sigma\acute{\iota}\alpha.$$

Note also the absence of Porson's bridge. In tragedy, the substitution of double breve for an anceps or a breve is found normally only at the beginning of a line. When it occurs elsewhere in the trimeter, it is to accommodate a proper name. It might be noted here that, generally, proper names are the worst offenders against metrical regularity.

Example: Sophocles, *Oedipus Coloneus* 1 :

$$T\acute{\epsilon}\kappa\nu o\nu \ \tau\upsilon\phi\lambda o\hat{\upsilon} \ \gamma\acute{\epsilon}\rho o\nu\tau o\varsigma \ '\!A\nu\tau\iota\gamma\acute{o}\nu\eta, \ \tau\acute{\iota}\nu\alpha\varsigma$$

But even in tragedy, resolution of at least one longum in the first or second metron is not uncommon.*

---

*The double breve substituted for one longum is rarely made up of the final and initial syllables of two different words. One exception: Eur. *Ion* 931.

Examples: Euripides, *Hippolytus* 614 and *Iphigenia Taurica* 79:

ἀπέπτυσ᾽· οὐδεὶς ἄδικός ἐστί μοι φίλος.
∪ — ∪ — — ∪∪∪ / — ∪ — ∪ — //

μητέρα κατακτάς, διαδοχαῖς δ᾽ Ἐρινύων
— ∪∪∪ — — / ∪∪∪ — ∪ — ∪ — //

Under this heading we may add the *choliamb*, also called the *scazon* ("limping"). It differs from the ordinary iambic trimeter in that a longum always replaces the last breve. In most examples of this verse, the third anceps is short. The first to use this meter extensively was Hipponax. Hence Callimachus begins his *Iambi* as follows (fr. 191 Pfeiffer 1–2):

Ἀκούσαθ᾽ Ἱππώνακτος· οὐ γὰρ ἀλλ᾽ ἥκω
∪ — ∪ — — — ∪ / — ∪ — — //

ἐκ τῶν ὅκου βοῦν κολλύβου πιπρήσκουσιν,
— — ∪ — — / — ∪ — ∪ — — — //

Because the ending of this period was felt to be twisted out of shape, the choliamb was widely used for invective and satire.

8. The Trochaic Tetrameter

The name "trochee" literally means "running". Though the trochaic tetrameter was occasionally used for the dialogue of drama, it was felt to be a less stately meter than the iambic trimeter.

The verse is divided by a diaeresis after two metra, but equality of the two parts is avoided by the catalectic ending which the period normally exhibits: 2 tro/2 tro$_\wedge$//. Bridges analogous to those of the tragic trimeter further define this unit:

— ∪ — ∪͡ — ∪ — x / — ∪ — ∪͡ — ∪ — //

Example: Archilochus fr. 67a D. 6:

ἀλλὰ χαρτοῖσίν τε χαῖρε καὶ κακοῖσιν ἀσχάλα
— ∪ — — — ∪ — ∪ / — ∪ — ∪ — ∪ — //

Resolution of a longum is permitted; where the second longum of a metron is resolved, the three final syllables of the metron are usually contained within the same word.

Example: Euripides, *Bacchae* 613:

ἀλλὰ πῶς ἠλευθερώθης ἀνδρὸς ἀνοσίου τυχών;
— ∪ — — — ∪ — — / — ∪ ∪ ∪ ∪— ∪ — //

In comedy, the central diaeresis is sometimes replaced by a caesura before the second anceps and the bridges are less closely observed. This helps to loosen up the set movement of the verse.

Example: Aristophanes, *Clouds* 1117:

πρῶτα μὲν γάρ, ἢν νεᾶν βούλησθ' ἐν ὥρᾳ τοὺς ἀγρούς,
— ∪ — ∪ — ∪ —/ — — ∪ — — — ∪ — //

9. Lyric Meters

The metrical varieties discussed in sections 5–8 pertain to non-lyrical or spoken verse, recited without the aid of musical instruments. This is true even of the hexameter; whatever its origins, in the classical period it was delivered without musical accompaniment. In what follows we shall treat of lyric or sung verse. While spoken verse usually consists of identically formed periods following one another in stichic sequence (κατὰ στίχον), sung verse is mostly grouped by strophes, each strophe consisting of several periods which may or may not be identical in form. The periods and metra forming a strophe usually produce the effect of a homogeneous or identifiable meter (Ionic, Aeolic, Dactylo-epitrite, etc.), and this is true also of the complete poem if it is composed of strophes, antistrophes, and epodes (cf. below, section 17). The only type of lyric poetry which does not conform to this rule of homogeneity is that which occurs in Attic drama (cf. below, section 18); in earlier poetry the mixing of meters seems to have been very rare.

10. Lyric Dactyls

The lyric dactyls (also known as "Doric dactyls") of early Greek poetry differ from the hexameter in three major respects.

1. Replacement of a double breve by a longum is less frequent. In Alcman and Stesichorus double breve is the norm, and dissyllabic dactyls are usually restricted to the first part of the period. Alcman's dactylic tetrameter runs roughly as follows:

$$- \overset{\frown}{\cup\cup} - \overset{\frown}{\cup\cup} - \cup\cup - \cup(\cup)/ \quad * \qquad 4 \text{ da}/$$

Note the bridge which prevents the verse from breaking in half.

Example: Alcman fr. 49 D. 1:

$$καί \ ποκά \ τοι \ δώσω \ τρίποδος \ κύτος,$$
$$- \ \cup \ \cup \ - \ - \ - \ \cup \ \cup \ - \ \cup \ \cup$$

The four dactylic hexameters of fr. 94 D. are trisyllabic throughout. In later poetry, however, a longum may be substituted even for the double breve of the third or fourth metron.

Example: Sophocles, *Electra* 238–240:

$$ἐν \ τίνι \ τοῦτ' \ ἔβλαστ' \ ἀνθρώπων;$$
$$- \ \cup \ \cup \ - \ - \ - \ - \ -$$

$$μήτ' \ εἴην \ ἔντιμος \ τούτοις$$

$$μήτ', \ εἴ \ τῳ \ πρόσκειμαι \ χρηστῷ,$$

2. The dactyls may be *rising*, i.e., the first longum of the period may be preceded by a longum or a double breve, occasionally also by a single breve. Confusion of such rising dactyls with anapaests (cf. below, section 11) is usually avoided by the position of the breaks.

---

* The parenthesis draws attention to the fact that the last breve is occasionally not represented; cf. the example from Ibycus p. 18 top.

Example: Ibycus fr. 7 D. 3:

κηλήμασι παντοδαποῖσ᾽ ἐς ἄπειρα   − 4 da_∧
$$- - \cup\cup - \cup\cup - \quad \cup\cup - \cup \qquad -4\ \mathrm{da}_\wedge$$

Note the absence of the diaeresis which we associate with the anapaestic dimeter. A further means of distinguishing rising dactyls from anapaests is to be found in the fact that, in the earlier writers at least, the longa of dactyls are almost never resolved.

3. The end of a dactylic series or period need not be $-\cup\cup--\|$ (notation: $2\ \mathrm{da}_\wedge\|$), but may terminate in a longum which does not complete the full metron. Such an ending is called *blunt* when the final longum is preceded by a breve, and *pendant* when the final longum is preceded by a longum. Of the three examples which follow, (a) and (b) show blunt ending, while (c) shows pendant ending.

(a) $-\cup\cup-\|$ (notation: $2\ \mathrm{da}_{\wedge\wedge}\|$).

Example: Ibycus fr. 7 D. 7:

$$\text{ἀέκων σὺν ὄχεσφι θοοῖσ᾽ ἐς ἄμιλλαν ἔβα.}$$
$$\cup\cup - \cup \ \cup - \cup\cup - \ \cup\cup - \cup \ \cup - \|$$

(b) $-\cup\cup-\cup-\|$ (notation: $2\ \mathrm{da}^{\cup\,-}\|$).

Example: Ibycus fr. 6 D. 8 (Wilamowitz' reading):

$$\langle\text{ἀλλ᾽ ἄ}\rangle\theta᾽\ \text{ὑπὸ στεροπᾶς φλέγων}$$
$$- \ \cup \ \cup - \ \cup\cup - \ - \|$$

(c) $-\cup\cup-\cup--\|$ (notation: $3\ \mathrm{da}_{\wedge\wedge}^{\cup\,-\,-}\|$).

Example: Ibycus fr. 6 D. 12 (Hesychius' reading):

$$\text{ἐγκρατέως πεδόθεν φυλάσσει}$$
$$- \ \cup\cup - \ \cup\cup - \cup \ - \ - \|$$

That this last clausula is dactylic is proved by the fact that in Alcman's *Partheneion* $-\cup\cup-\cup--\|\|\|$ responds * to $-\cup\cup-\cup\cup-\|\|\|$.

* The term *responsion* refers to the parallelism of metric schemes between strophe and strophe or strophe and antistrophe.

Example: col. ii lines 1 and 15 Page:

Ϝέργα πάθον κακὰ μησαμένοι.
— ∪ ∪ — ∪ ∪ — ∪ ∪ — ///

τῶν ὑποπετριδίων ὀνείρων.
— ∪ ∪ — ∪ ∪ — ∪ — — ///

It appears, then, that this particular clausula has both a blunt and a pendant form; the element preceding the final longum is an anceps (notation: $4\,\mathrm{da}_{\wedge\wedge}^{\vee\times}\,—///$)). This anceps–longum termination confirms the general rule that at the end of the period Greek verse shows greater metrical license than within the period (cf. also *brevis in longo*, above, section 3. 3), and that at the end of a strophe, where this sequence is often found, the desire for an emphatic ending provides an added incentive for metrical freedom.

Lyric dactyls are prominent in Alcman, Stesichorus, and Ibycus. Pindar and Bacchylides use them sparingly, except as elements in more complex meters such as Dactylo-epitrites and Dactylo-iambics (cf. below, section 17. 2–3). The kinship between lyric dactyls and Dactylo-epitrites is clear from such a poem as Stesichorus fr. 17 D. whose first two lines may be analyzed either as dactyls or as Dactylo-epitrites:

οὕνεκα Τυνδάρεος $3\,\mathrm{da}_{\wedge\wedge} = D$
— ∪ ∪ — ∪ ∪ —

ῥέζων ποτὲ πᾶσι θεοῖς μούνας λάθετ᾽ ἠπιοδώρου
— — ∪ ∪ — ∪ ∪ — — — ∪ ∪ — ∪∪ — —
                              $- 6\,\mathrm{da}_{\wedge} = -D{-}D{-}$

After the archaic period, lyric dactyls remain important especially in cult poetry; witness the popular *Hymn to Asclepius* (J. U. Powell, *Collectanea Alexandr.* (Oxford 1925) 136), composed ca. 400 B.C. In drama, dactylic odes create an effect of hieratic stateliness; cf. Aeschylus, *Agamemnon*

104 ff., Aristophanes, *Clouds* 275 ff., and especially Sophocles, *Oedipus Coloneus* 229 ff.:

οὐδενὶ μοιριδία τίσις ἔρχεται
— ∪ ∪ — ∪ ∪— ∪ ∪ — ∪ ∪

ὧν προπάθῃ τὸ τίνειν· ἀπάτα δ᾽ ἀπά-
— ∪ ∪ — ∪ ∪ — ∪ ∪ — ∪ ∪

ταις ἑτέραις ἑτέρα παραβαλλομέ-
— ∪ ∪ — ∪ ∪— ∪ ∪ — ∪ ∪

να πόνον, οὐ χάριν, ἀντιδίδωσιν ἔχειν.
— ∪ ∪ — ∪ ∪ — ∪ ∪— ∪ ∪ —

Note that it would be possible to divide the lines differently, and to start lines 231 and 232 with rising dactyls. In fact, the dactylic units follow one another so smoothly that any line division will do an injustice to the rhythm.

11. Anapaests

In this meter, longum and double breve are equivalent; one may replace the other without straining the rhythmic sequence, for in an anapaestic period a longum is exactly double the value of two brevia. Hence the rhythm of anapaests is firm and regular, suitable for the musical setting of marches and processionals. By the same token, the end of each metron tends to coincide with a word ending; only in the catalectic dimeter (*paroemiac* = "proverbial") at the end of an anapaestic period or strophe is diaeresis less frequent. The scheme of the anapaestic tetrameter, consisting of a dimeter and a paroemiac, is as follows:

$$\overline{\cup\cup} \; \overset{\cup\cup}{—} \; \overline{\cup\cup} \; \overset{\cup\cup}{—} / \overline{\cup\cup} \; \overset{\cup\cup}{—} \; \overline{\cup\cup} \; \overset{\cup\cup}{—} / \overline{\cup\cup} \; \overset{\cup\cup}{—} \; \overline{\overset{\frown}{\cup\cup}} \; — \cup\cup — —//$$

$$4 \; an_\wedge //$$

except that cases of four consecutive brevia are rare. This structure is found in its purest form in the anapaestic parodi of tragedy and in some of the parabases of comedy.

Example from tragedy: Aeschylus, *Suppliants* 12–13:

καὶ στασίαρχος τάδε πεσσονομῶν κύδιστ' ἀχέων ἐπέκρινεν
— ∪ ∪— —/ ∪ ∪ — ∪∪ — / — — ∪ ∪— ∪∪ — —//

Example from comedy: Aristophanes, *Peace* 729:

ἀλλ' ἴθι χαίρων· ἡμεῖς δὲ τέως τάδε τὰ σκεύη παραδόντες
— ∪∪ — — / — — ∪ ∪—/ ∪∪ — — — — ∪ ∪ — —//

Comedy also uses the anapaestic tetrameter catalectic as a verse of dialogue.

Example: Aristophanes, *Clouds* 268:

τὸ δὲ μηδὲ κυνῆν οἴκοθεν ἐλθεῖν ἐμὲ τὸν κακοδαίμον' ἔχοντα.
∪ ∪ — ∪ ∪ —/— ∪∪ — —/∪ ∪ — ∪ ∪— ∪ ∪ —--//

The chief difference between tragedy and comedy in the handling of anapaests is that in a tragic period any number of dimeters may precede the paroemiac, whereas comedy prefers stichic sequences of dimeter + paroemiac (4 an_∧//).

When anapaestic series are used in lyrical passages the meter is handled more freely. There is a greater accumulation of longs or shorts, periods may end without catalexis, and conversely catalexis may occur within a period.

Example: Euripides, *Ion* 151–155:

εἴθ' οὕτως αἰεὶ Φοίβῳ	2 an_∧ /
λατρεύων μὴ παυσαίμαν,	2 an_∧ /
ἢ παυσαίμαν ἀγαθᾷ μοίρᾳ.	2 an //
ἔα ἔα·	
φοιτῶσ' ἤδη λείπουσίν τε	2 an /
πτανοὶ Παρνασοῦ κοίτας·	2 an_∧ //

12. Lyric Iambs and Trochees

Lyric iambs and trochees are very common in drama, where they are usually mixed with their own truncated forms, i.e., cretics (— ◡ —) and bacchiacs (◡ — —).* Resolution of the longum into double breve is as common in lyric iambs and trochees as it is in their spoken equivalents.

Example: Sophocles, *Oedipus Rex* 179:

ὧν πόλις ἀνάριθμος ὄλλυται·   2 ia /
— ◡ ◡ ◡◡ ◡ — ◡ — /

Example of bacchiac clausula: *Oedipus Rex* 192:

φλέγει με περιβόατος ἀντιάζων,
◡ — ◡ ◡ ◡◡ — ◡ — ◡ — — //
3 ia‸ // or 2 ia ba //

Outside of drama, also, lyric iambs and trochees are rarely used in their pure form, though Alcman (see fr. 56 D.) and perhaps Simonides seem to have written entire periods and strophes consisting of or dominated by iambs, and Anacreon fr. 88 D. (cf. also 90 D.) consists wholly of trochees:

Πῶλε Θρηκίη, τί δή με λοξὸν ὄμμασι⟨ν⟩ βλέπουσα 4 tro//
— ◡ — ◡ — ◡ — ◡ / — ◡ — ◡ — ◡ — —//

νηλεῶς φεύγεις; δοκεῖς δέ μ' οὐδὲν εἰδέναι σοφόν.
— ◡ — — — ◡ — ◡ / — ◡ — ◡ — ◡ — ///
2 tro/ 2 tro‸ ///

Usually iambs or trochees help to complete a sequence of another character, mostly Ionic or Aeolic (cf. below, sections 13 and 16). In such cases they may, at the beginning or the end of a period, appear in truncated form.

Example of initial trochaic unit: Sappho fr. 1 LP 1:

Ποικιλόθρον' ἀθανάτ'Ἀφρόδιτα,   cr ‸hipp //
— ◡ — ◡ — ◡◡ — ◡ — —//

Example of final iambic unit: Anacreon fr. 45 D. 1:

Μεγάλῳ δηὖτέ μ' Ἔρως ἔκοψεν ὥστε χαλκεὺς
◡ ◡ — — ◡ ◡ — ◡ — ◡ — ◡ — —//

◡◡— cho ia ba //

---

* When cretics or bacchiacs appear in resolved form, they are sometimes referred to as *paeons*. First paeon: — ◡ ◡ ◡; fourth paeon: ◡ ◡ ◡ —.

Other iambic or trochaic forms used widely with Ionic or Aeolic meters are the *lecythion:* $- \cup - \times - \cup -$ and the *ithyphallic:* $- \cup - \cup - -$.

Anacreon fr. 54 D. is an interesting example of the generous use of iambs in an Ionic system. Note the responsion of choriamb and iamb in lines 1 and 7, i.e., the first lines of strophe 1 and 3 respectively:

Πρὶν μὲν ἔχων βερβέριον, καλύμματ᾽ ἐσφηκωμένα,
$\underline{\quad} \ \cup \ \cup \ \underline{\quad} \underline{\quad} \cup \cup \underline{\quad} \ \cup \ \underline{\quad} \ \cup \ \underline{\quad} \underline{\quad} \underline{\quad} \cup \underline{\quad} //$

2 cho / 2 ia //

πολλὰ μὲν ἐν δουρὶ τιθεὶς αὐχένα, πολλὰ δ᾽ ἐν τροχῷ,
$\underline{\quad} \ \cup \ \cup \ \underline{\quad} \underline{\quad} \cup \cup \underline{\quad} \underline{\quad} \cup \cup \ \underline{\quad} \ \cup \ \underline{\quad} \ \cup \ \underline{\quad} //$

3 cho ia //

13. Ionic Meters

Ionics and choriambs are the only basic metra (i.e., metra consisting of from three to six elements each) which do not occur in spoken verse. We have specimens of pure ionic structures by Alcman (fr. 34 D.), Sappho (fr. 135 LP), Alcaeus (fr. A 10 LP), Anacreon and others, including the dramatists.

Example: Aeschylus, *Persians* 93–96:

δολόμητιν δ᾽ ἀπάταν θεοῦ τίς ἀνὴρ θνατὸς ἀλύξει;   4 io //
$\cup \ \cup \underline{\quad} \underline{\quad} \ \underline{\quad} \ \cup \ \cup \underline{\quad} \ \underline{\quad} \ \cup \ \cup \underline{\quad} \ \cup \ \cup \underline{\quad} //$

τίς ὁ κραιπνῷ ποδὶ πηδήματος εὐπετέος ἀνάσσων;   4 io //
$\cup \ \cup \underline{\quad} \ \underline{\quad} \ \cup \ \cup \underline{\quad} \underline{\quad} \ \cup \ \cup \ \underline{\quad} \ \cup \cup \cup \ \cup \underline{\quad} \ \underline{\quad} //$

A catalectic ionic tetrameter is called *galliambic*. It is first found in Phrynichus.

Example: fr. 14 Nauck:

τό γε μὴν ξείνια δούσαις, λόγος ὥσπερ λέγεται   4 io_∧ //
$\cup \ \cup \ \underline{\quad} \ \ \underline{\quad} \cup \cup \ \underline{\quad} \ \underline{\quad} \ \ \cup \ \cup \ \underline{\quad} \ \underline{\quad} \ \cup \cup \ \underline{\quad} //$

A later form of the galliambic, with free use of resolution and substitution of longum for double breve, is found in a frag-

23

ment which has come down under the name of Callimachus, fr. 761 Pfeiffer:

Γάλλαι μητρὸς ὀρείης φιλόθυρσοι δρομάδες, 4 io‿ //
— ‿ — ‿ ‿ — — ‿ ‿ — — ‿ ‿ — //

αἷς ἔντεα παταγεῖται καὶ χάλκεα κρόταλα 4 io‿ //
— — ‿‿ ‿ ‿ — — — — — ‿‿ ‿ ‿ — //

Choriambs also may be used by themselves to form a complete system, often with final bacchiac for clausula.

Example: Sappho fr. 128 LP:

δεῦτέ νυν ἅβραι Χάριτες καλλίκομοί τε Μοῖσαι 3 cho ba //
— ‿ ‿ — — ‿ ‿ — — ‿ ‿ — ‿ — — //

In Sappho and particularly in Anacreon, as also in later uses of the galliambic (cf. the Latin adaptation of Catullus, *c.* 63), an ionic dimeter with the fourth and fifth elements reversed is popular. It is called *anaclast* (from the Greek ἀνάκλασις = "bending back") and may be used by itself or in combination with ionics, choriambs, or dactyls.

Example of anaclast alone: Anacreon fr. 44 D. 1–2:

Πολιοὶ μὲν ἡμὶν ἤδη anacl /
‿ ‿ — ‿ — ‿ — — /

κρόταφοι κάρη τε λευκόν, anacl /
‿ ‿ — ‿ — ‿ — — /

Anacreon's ionic trimeters of frs. 36–42 D. have the form:

‿ ‿ — ‿̄ —̄ ‿ ‿ — ‿̄ —̄ ‿ ‿ — — .

The three possible versions appear side by side in the three lines of fr. 39 D.:

ἀγανῶς οἷά τε νεβρὸν νεοθηλέα 3 io /
‿ ‿ — — ‿ ‿ — — ‿‿ — /

γαλαθηνόν, ὅς τ' ἐν ὕλῃ κεροέσσης anacl io /
‿ ‿ — ‿ — — ‿ ‿— — /

ἀπολειφθεὶς ἀπὸ μητρὸς ἐπτοήθη io anacl /
‿ ‿ — — ‿ ‿ — ‿ — ‿— — /

24

ment which has come down under the name of Callimachus, fr. 761 Pfeiffer:

Γάλλαι μητρὸς ὀρείης φιλόθυρσοι δρομάδες,   4 io_∧ //
‾ ‾ ‾ ᵕ ᵕ ‾ ‾ ᵕ ᵕ ‾ ‾ ᵕ ᵕ ‾ //

αἷς ἔντεα παταγεῖται καὶ χάλκεα κρόταλα   4 io_∧ //
‾ ‾ ᵕᵕ ᵕ ᵕ ‾ ‾ ‾ ‾ ᵕᵕ ᵕ ᵕ ‾ //

Choriambs also may be used by themselves to form a complete system, often with final bacchiac for clausula.

Example: Sappho fr. 128 LP:

δεῦτέ νυν ἄβραι Χάριτες καλλίκομοί τε Μοῖσαι 3 cho ba //
‾ᵕ ᵕ ‾ ‾ ᵕ ᵕ‾ ‾ ᵕ ᵕ ‾ ᵕ ‾ ‾//

In Sappho and particularly in Anacreon, as also in later uses of the galliambic (cf. the Latin adaptation of Catullus, *c.* 63), an ionic dimeter with the fourth and fifth elements reversed is popular. It is called *anaclast* (from the Greek ἀνάκλασις = "bending back") and may be used by itself or in combination with ionics, choriambs, or dactyls.

Example of anaclast alone: Anacreon fr. 44 D. 1–2:

Πολιοὶ μὲν ἡμὶν ἤδη   anacl /
ᵕ ᵕ ‾ ᵕ ‾ ᵕ ‾ ‾ /

κρόταφοι κάρη τε λευκόν,   anacl /
ᵕ ᵕ ‾ ᵕ ‾ ᵕ ‾ ‾ /

Anacreon's ionic trimeters of frs. 36–42 D. have the form:

ᵕ ᵕ ‾ ᵘ̱ ‾ᵘ ᵕ ‾ ᵘ̱ ‾ᵘ ᵕ ‾ ‾.

The three possible versions appear side by side in the three lines of fr. 39 D.:

ἀγανῶς οἷά τε νεβρὸν νεοθηλέα   3 io /
ᵕ ᵕ ‾ ‾ᵕ ᵕ ‾ ‾ ᵕ ᵕ‾ ‾/

γαλαθηνόν, ὅς τ' ἐν ὕλῃ κεροέσσης anacl io /
ᵕ ᵕ ‾ ᵕ ‾ ‾ ᵕ ᵕ‾ ‾/

ἀπολειφθεὶς ἀπὸ μητρὸς ἐπτοήθη io anacl /
ᵕ ᵕ ‾ ‾ ᵕ ᵕ ‾ ᵕ ‾ ᵕ‾ ‾/

24

Other iambic or trochaic forms used widely with Ionic or Aeolic meters are the *lecythion:* $- \cup - \times - \cup -$ and the *ithyphallic:* $- \cup - \cup - -$.

Anacreon fr. 54 D. is an interesting example of the generous use of iambs in an Ionic system. Note the responsion of choriamb and iamb in lines 1 and 7, i.e., the first lines of strophe 1 and 3 respectively:

Πρὶν μὲν ἔχων βερβέριον, καλύμματ᾽ ἐσφηκωμένα,
$- \cup \cup - - \cup \cup - \cup - \cup - - \cup - //$
2 cho / 2 ia //

πολλὰ μὲν ἐν δουρὶ τιθεὶς αὐχένα, πολλὰ δ᾽ ἐν τροχῷ,
$- \cup \cup - - \cup \cup - - \cup \cup - \cup - \cup - //$
3 cho ia //

13. Ionic Meters

Ionics and choriambs are the only basic metra (i.e., metra consisting of from three to six elements each) which do not occur in spoken verse. We have specimens of pure ionic structures by Alcman (fr. 34 D.), Sappho (fr. 135 LP), Alcaeus (fr. A 10 LP), Anacreon and others, including the dramatists.

Example: Aeschylus, *Persians* 93–96:

δολόμητιν δ᾽ ἀπάταν θεοῦ τίς ἀνὴρ θνατὸς ἀλύξει; 4 io //
$\cup \cup - - \cup \cup - - \cup \cup - \cup - \cup - - //$

τίς ὁ κραιπνῷ ποδὶ πηδήματος εὐπετέος ἀνάσσων; 4 io //
$\cup \cup - - \cup \cup - - \cup \cup - \cup \cup \cup - - //$

A catalectic ionic tetrameter is called *galliambic*. It is first found in Phrynichus.

Example: fr. 14 Nauck:

τό γε μὴν ξείνια δούσαις, λόγος ὥσπερ λέγεται 4 io∧ //
$\cup \cup - - \cup \cup - - \cup \cup - - \cup \cup - //$

A later form of the galliambic, with free use of resolution and substitution of longum for double breve, is found in a frag-

23

Sappho fr. 102 LP is an example of anaclast used in combination with iambic rhythm:

γλύκηα μᾶτερ, οὔτοι δύναμαι κρέκην τὸν ἴστον
˘ — ˘ — ˘ — — / ˘ ˘ — ˘ — ˘ — — /

ia ba / anacl /

There is a close relation between Ionic and Aeolic meters (for Aeolic, cf. below, section 16) which emerges most strikingly from the existence of a unit known as *polyschematist:* × × — × — ˘ ˘ —. This is not a choriambic dimeter, since the elements preceding the final choriamb tend to exhibit many resolutions and may form almost anything *but* a choriamb. But see Eur. *Orestes* 839.

Example: Euripides, *Ion* 1053:

πότνια πότνι᾿ ἐμὰ χθονίας   polysch
˘ ˘ ˘ ˘ ˘ ˘ — ˘ ˘ —

The polyschematist occurs mostly in Attic drama and in Corinna, often in combination with Aeolic meters such as the glyconic (× × — ˘ ˘ — ˘ —). The following fragment of Corinna (fr. 4 Page) uses a sequence of uniform polyschematists:

καλὰ Ϝέροι᾿ ἀϊσομένα
˘ ˘ — ˘ — ˘ — /

Ταναγρίδεσσι λευκοπέπλοις.
˘ ˘ ˘ ˘ — ˘ — ˘ — //

μέγα δ᾿ ἐμὰ γέγαθε πόλις
˘ ˘ — ˘ — ˘ — /

λιγυροκωτίλαισ᾿ ἐνοπαῖς.
˘ ˘ ˘ — ˘ — ˘ ˘ — //

Finally it should be mentioned that recent papyrus finds of Anacreon have shown that Ionic meters could be handled rather more freely than the fragments hitherto known had led us to believe. Note the anaclast of the form ˘ ˘ — — — ˘ — — part of which has turned up in *Oxyrhynchus Papyri* No. 2321. 4:

· · · ῳ πολλὴν ὀφείλω
— — — ˘ — —

Further finds will no doubt enrich our knowledge of the variations of this as well as other meters.

14. Complex Lyric Meters

The periods discussed in sections 5–13 are generally composed of the basic metra, each of them consisting of from three to six elements, or of their derivatives or truncated forms. There are, however, many structures whose periods it is impossible to reduce to the regular sequence of basic metra. Sappho fr. 102 LP, cited above, section 13, is an example of a complex metrical structure, in this case composed of iambic and ionic elements. The first to put together such complex metrical structures was Archilochus, in the poems which fall under the next heading.

15. Epodes and Asynarteta

In making up his complex systems, Archilochus draws on dactylic hexameters, iambic trimeters (both acatalectic and catalectic), iambic dimeters, structures derived from the hexameter such as the hemiepes (see above, section 6), and the *enoplion* which is roughly the part of the hexameter following the caesura after the third longum:

$$ x - \widebreve{\cup\cup} - \cup\cup -- / $$

Further, he draws on the dactylic tetrameter, the lecythion, and the ithyphallic (cf. above, section 12). The components are joined together in the following manner:

1. A longer sequence is followed by a shorter sequence, with a pause to separate them: a//b//a//b//a//b//. . . . This type of combination is called an *epode* (not to be confused with the epode of choral poetry, cf. below, sections 17 and 18).

26

Example: Archilochus fr. 104 D. 2–3:

ἄψυχος, χαλεπῆσι θεῶν ὀδύνῃσιν ἕκητι   6 da_∧ //

πεπαρμένος δι' ὀστέων.   2 ia //

Another example: Callimachus, *Iambi* 7 (fr. 197 Pfeiffer) 1–2:

Ἑρμᾶς ὁ Περφεραῖος, Αἰνίων θεός,   3 ia //

ἔμμι τῶ φυγαίχμα   ith //

2. A longer sequence is followed by a shorter sequence, without pause but with a diaeresis between them: a/b//a/b//. ... This type of combination is called an *asynarteton* ("not joined together").

Example: Archilochus fr. 109 D.:

ἀστῶν δ' οἱ μὲν κατόπισθεν   enopl /

ἦσαν, οἱ δὲ πολλοί   ith //

Another example: Callimachus, *Iambi* 5 (fr. 195 Pfeiffer) 31–32:

ἐγὼ Βάκις τοι καὶ Σίβυλλα [καὶ] δάφνη   chol /

καὶ φηγός. ἀλλὰ συμβαλεῦ   2 ia //

3. An asynarteton may be followed by a third sequence, with the whole constituting an expanded type of epode: a/b//c//a/b//c//a/b//c//. ...

Example: Archilochus fr. 112 D. 1–2:

τοῖος γὰρ φιλότητος ἔρως ὑπὸ καρδίην ἐλυσθείς 4 da / ith //

πολλὴν κατ' ἀχλὺν ὀμμάτων ἔχευεν   3 ia_∧ //

27

Another example: Theocritus, *Epigrams* 21. 1–3:

Ἀρχίλοχον καὶ στῆθι καὶ εἴσιδε τὸν πάλαι ποιητὴν 4 da / ith //
— ∪∪ — — — ∪ ∪ — ∪∪/— ∪ — ∪——//

τὸν τῶν ἰάμβων, οὗ τὸ μυρίον κλέος   3 ia //
— — ∪ — — — ∪ — ∪— ∪ —//

διῆλθε κἠπὶ νύκτα καὶ πρὸς ἠῶ.   3 ia∧ //
∪ — ∪ — ∪ — ∪ — ∪ ——//

The examples cited show that the writing of epodes and
asynarteta was as popular in the Hellenistic age as it had
been in the archaic. Most of the combinations used by the
Alexandrians and the Greco-Roman writers had been
established by Archilochus and his immediate successors,
but there were a few new forms. The *Meliambics* ("sung
iambics", but, like most lyric meters adopted by the
Alexandrians, they were recited rather than sung) of
Cercidas, for instance, combine dactylic components (he-
miepes and enoplion) and iambic components (lecythion
and × — ∪ — ×) in a distinctive manner.

Example: p. 145 lines 8–10 D.:

τοῖς δὲ τὰν ἀριστερὰν λύσας ἐπόρσῃ
— ∪ — ∪— ∪ —/— — ∪ — —//

λαίλαπας ἢ λαμυρὰς πόθων ἀέλλας,
— ∪ ∪ — ∪ ∪ —/ ∪ — ∪— —//

κυματίας δι' ὅλου τούτοις ὁ πορθμός.
— ∪ ∪— ∪ ∪ —/ — — ∪ — —//

Some asynarteta became more popular than others. Take
the verse — ∪∪ — ∪∪ —/× — ∪ ——// which is used in the last
two lines of the quotation from Cercidas. An early example
of it occurs in Alcaeus fr. Z 60 LP:

ἦρ' ἔτι Διννομένη τὼ Τυρρακήω
— ∪∪ — ∪∪—/ — — ∪ ——//

τάρμενα λάμπρα κέοντ' ἐν Μυρσινήῳ;
— ∪∪ — ∪ ∪— /— — ∪——//

The ancient metricians called it the *encomiologicus*, i.e., the
meter employed in songs of praise, and felt that it consisted
of the first part of the hexameter and the first part of the

iambic trimeter. Later Anacreon takes up this meter, but with the modification that the word ending may occur after the anceps rather than between the two sections:

$$- \cup \cup - \cup \cup - \mid \times \mid - \cup - - \mid\mid .$$

Example: fr. 65 D. 2-3:

πάντας, ⟨ὅσ⟩οι χθονίους ἔχουσι ῥυσμοὺς
$$- \cup \ - \ \cup - \ \cup \cup \ - \mid \cup - \cup - \ \ - \mid\mid$$

καὶ χαλεπούς. μεμάθηκά σ', ὦ Μεγίστη,
$$- \cup \cup \ - \ \cup \cup - \cup \ \mid - \ \cup - \ - \mid\mid$$

With the break less uniformly located, the meter may be analyzed as an early form of Dactylo-epitrite (cf. below, section 17. 2). In this new arrangement, the character of the original components, if indeed they were what the ancient metricians thought they were, came to be effectively disguised. According to some modern scholars many of the bridges operative in the classical Greek meters were designed to hide the seams or joints of the original combinations.

16. Aeolic Meters

Aeolic meters are distinguished from all others by two characteristics:

1. The so-called "choriambic" nucleus of the verse ("so-called", because the $- \cup \cup -$ of Aeolic meters has little to do with the choriamb) is preceded by the *Aeolic base*, consisting of two ancipitia which do not follow the rules of responsion, i.e., a longum may respond to a breve and vice versa.

2. After the base, no longum may be replaced by two brevia, nor may two brevia be replaced by a longum.

Thus, in an Aeolic metron the number of syllables and, after the base, the quantities of the syllables, are rigidly fixed.*

* In Anacreon, Pindar and Attic drama, Aeolic longa may be resolved. This infraction of one of the basic rules applying to Aeolic heralds the mixing of meters which was to be the hallmark of dramatic lyric poetry; cf. below, section 18.

The chief Aeolic meters are: the *glyconic:* × × — ∪ ∪ — ∪ —.

Example: Anacreon fr. 1 D. 1:

$$Γουνοῦμαί\ σ',\ ἐλαφηβόλε,$$
— — —   ∪ ∪ — ∪ — ||

The *pherecratean* (a catalectic glyconic): × × — ∪ ∪ — —.

Example: Anacreon fr. 1 D. 3:

$$δέσποιν'\ "Αρτεμι\ θηρῶν,$$
— — — ∪ ∪ — — ||

The *hipponactean* (a hypermetric glyconic): × × — ∪ ∪ — ∪ — —.

Example: Alcman fr. 18 D.:

$$ὢς\ ἁμὲς\ τὸ\ καλὸν\ μελίσκον$$
— — — ∪ ∪ — ∪ — — ||

It will be seen from this that the glyconic is the basic Aeolic meter. With the glyconic compare also the polyschematist discussed in section 13. They are similar in form, though the polyschematist is a much freer verse, and they may be used in combination.

Example: Euripides, *Ion* 1066–1068:

$$πάθεσι\ πάθεα\ δ'\ ἐξανύτουσ'$$ polysch /
∪ ∪ ∪   ∪ ∪ ∪   — ∪ ∪   — /

$$εἰς\ ἄλλας\ βιότου\ κάτεισι\ μορφάς.$$ gl ba //
— — — ∪∪ — ∪ — ∪ — — //

When the glyconic and the pherecratean are combined into one period, the resulting structure is called *priapean.*

Example: Anacreon fr. 69 D. 1:

$$ἠρίστησα\ μὲν\ ἰτρίου\ λεπτοῦ\ μικρὸν\ ἀποκλάς,$$
— — — ∪   ∪   — ∪ — /— — —   ∪ ∪   — — //

Finally it should be mentioned that all three Aeolic meters also occur in acephalous form, i.e., with monosyllabic base. A combination of ˄gl (also called *telesilleion*) and ˄ph (also called *reizianum*) is to be seen in Aristophanes, *Knights* 1111–1114:

$$\underset{-\ -\ \cup\ \ \cup\ -\ \ \cup\ -}{\mathring{\omega}\ \varDelta \hat{\eta}\mu\epsilon\ \kappa\alpha\lambda\acute{\eta}\nu\ \gamma'\ \mathring{\epsilon}\chi\epsilon\iota\varsigma}\qquad\qquad {}_{\wedge}\mathrm{gl}$$

$$\underset{-\ -\ \cup\ \cup\ -\ \cup\ -}{\mathring{\alpha}\rho\chi\acute{\eta}\nu,\ \mathring{o}\tau\epsilon\ \pi\acute{\alpha}\nu\tau\epsilon\varsigma\ \mathring{\alpha}\nu\text{-}}\qquad\qquad {}_{\wedge}\mathrm{gl}$$

$$\underset{-\ -\ \cup\ \cup\ -\ \cup\ -}{\theta\rho\omega\pi o\iota\ \delta\epsilon\delta\acute{\iota}\alpha\sigma\acute{\iota}\ \sigma'\ \mathring{\omega}\sigma\text{-}}\qquad\qquad {}_{\wedge}\mathrm{gl}$$

$$\underset{-\ -\ \cup\ \cup\ -\ -\ //}{\pi\epsilon\rho\ \mathring{\alpha}\nu\delta\rho\alpha\ \tau\acute{\upsilon}\rho\alpha\nu\nu o\nu.}\qquad\qquad {}_{\wedge}\mathrm{ph}\ //$$

In the early lyric, such series of pure Aeolic meters are rare. Usually, Aeolic meters occur in compound form. Here we distinguish between *external* and *internal compounding*.

In external compounding, we often find the meters combined, initially or finally, with full or truncated iambs or trochees (see above, section 12). The position of the ancipitia (or, in the case of acephaly, of the anceps) of the Aeolic base serves to indicate the presence of initial compounding. Thus, the so-called Sapphic hendecasyllable, i.e., the first or second line of the Sapphic strophe, may be analyzed as follows: cr ${}_{\wedge}$hipp//.

Example: Sappho fr. 1 LP lines 1 and 5:

$$\underset{-\ \cup\ \cup\ -\ \cup\ \cup\ -\ -\ //}{\Pi o\iota\kappa\iota\lambda\acute{o}\theta\rho o\nu'\ \mathring{\alpha}\theta\alpha\nu\acute{\alpha}\tau'A\phi\rho\acute{o}\delta\iota\tau\alpha}$$

$$\underset{-\ \cup\ -\ \ -\ -\ \cup\ \cup\ -\ \cup\ -\ -\ //}{\mathring{\alpha}\lambda\lambda\grave{\alpha}\ \tau\upsilon\acute{\iota}\delta'\ \mathring{\epsilon}\lambda\theta',\ \alpha\H{\iota}\ \pi o\tau\alpha\ \kappa\mathring{\alpha}\tau\acute{\epsilon}\rho\omega\tau\alpha}$$

Note that the fourth syllable is an anceps; this marks the position of the base. Again, in the third period of the so-called first Alcaic strophe, an acephalous Aeolic meter is preceded by two iambs.

Example: Alcaeus fr. D 14 LP lines 5–6 and 9–10:

$$\underset{-\ \ -\ \cup\ \ -\ \ -\ \cup\ \cup\ -\ \cup\ \ \cup\ \ -\ ///}{\kappa\alpha\grave{\iota}\ \nu\acute{\upsilon}\kappa\tau\iota\ \pi\alpha\phi\lambda\acute{\alpha}\sigma\delta\epsilon\iota\ \ldots\ \alpha\chi\theta\epsilon\nu,\ \mathring{\epsilon}\nu\theta\alpha\ \nu\acute{o}\mu o\varsigma\ \theta\acute{\alpha}\mu'\ \mathring{\epsilon}\nu\ \ldots\ \nu\eta\nu.}$$

$$\text{2ia }{}_{\wedge}\text{hipp}^{\mathrm{d}}\ ///*$$

$$\underset{-\ \ -\ \ \cup\ -\ -\ -\cup\ -\ \ -\ \ -\ \cup\ \cup\ -\ \ \cup\ \cup\ -\ -\ ///}{\pi\alpha\acute{\iota}\sigma\alpha\iota\varsigma\ \gamma\grave{\alpha}\rho\ \mathring{o}\nu\nu\acute{\omega}\rho\iota\nu\epsilon\ \nu\acute{\upsilon}\kappa\tau\alpha\varsigma,\ \tau\grave{\omega}\ \delta\grave{\epsilon}\ \pi\acute{\iota}\theta\omega\ \pi\alpha\tau\acute{\alpha}\gamma\epsilon\sigma\kappa'\ \mathring{o}\ \pi\acute{\upsilon}\theta\mu\eta\nu.}$$

$$\text{2ia }{}_{\wedge}\text{hipp}^{\mathrm{d}}\ ///$$

* For explanation of ${}^{\mathrm{d}}$ see the following note.

THE METERS OF GREEK AND LATIN POETRY

For an example of final compounding see Euripides, *Ion* 1067–1068, cited above, where a glyconic is completed by a bacchiac. In Alcaeus fr. Z 34 LP 7, two glyconics are followed by an iamb:

πὰρ δὲ Χαλκίδικαι σπάθαι, πὰρ δὲ ζώματα πόλλα καὶ κυπάσσιδες.
— ∪ — ∪∪ — ∪ —/ — — — ∪∪ — ∪ — ∪— ∪ —‖

            2 gl ia ‖

Twelve of the so-called *scolia*, i.e., drinking songs, quoted by Athenaeus, *Deipnosophistae* 15. 694 C ff., are composed largely of externally compounded Aeolic meters. Here is one *example*:

Πλούτου μητέρ' 'Ολυμπίαν ἀείδω   gl ba ‖
— — — ∪ — ∪ — ∪ — — ‖

Δήμητρα στεφανηφόροις ἐν ὥραις,   gl ba ‖
— — — ∪∪ — ∪ — ∪ — — ‖

σέ τε, παῖ Διός, Φερσεφόνη.   ∪∪—∪— ch ‖
∪ ∪ — ∪ — — ∪ ∪ — ‖

χαίρετον, εὖ δὲ τάνδ' ἀμφέπετον πόλιν.   ch gl ‖‖
— ∪ ∪ — ∪ — — ∪ ∪ — ∪ —‖‖

Internal compounding is accomplished by a repetition of the internal "choriamb" or, as in the case of Alcaeus fr. D 14 LP cited above, by a repetition of the internal "dactyl". That is to say, the three or four elements following upon the base are repeated at least once before the line is brought to its conclusion. For instance, repetition of the internal "dactyl" results in yet another type of hendecasyllable.

Example: Sappho fr. 131 LP:

"Ατθι, σοὶ δ' ἔμεθεν μὲν ἀπήχθετο   gl^d‖*
— ∪ — ∪ ∪ — ∪ — ∪ — ‖

φροντίσδην, ἐπὶ δ' 'Ανδρομέδαν πόται   gl^d‖
— — — ∪∪ — ∪ ∪ — ∪ —‖

The *asclepiadean* results from a repetition of the "choriamb".

* ^c or ^d in raised position indicates the repetition of a "choriamb" or a "dactyl" for internal compounding.

32

Example: Alcaeus fr. Z 27 LP 1–2:

ἦλθες ἐκ περάτων γᾶς ἐλεφαντίναν   gl^c//
‿ ‿ — ‿‿ — — ‿‿— ‿ —//

λάβαν τὼ ξίφεος χρυσοδέταν ἔχων   gl^c//
‿ — — ‿‿— — ‿‿ — ‿ —//

Compare also its catalectic form in Aristophanes, *Knights* 559–560:

δεῦρ᾽ ἔλθ᾽ ἐς χορὸν ὦ χρυσοτρίαιν᾽ ὦ   ph^c/
— — — ‿‿ ‿ ‿ — ‿ ‿ — —/

δελφίνων μεδέων Σουνιάρατε,   ph^c//
— — — ‿ ‿— — ‿ ‿——//

The *major asclepiadean* results from the addition of two "choriambs".

Example: Alcaeus fr. Z 23 LP 1–2:

τέγγε πλεύμονας οἴνῳ, τὸ γὰρ ἄστρον περιτέλλεται,   gl^{2c}//
—— — ‿ ‿ — — ‿ ‿ — — ‿‿ —‿ —//

ἀ δ᾽ ὥρα χαλέπα, πάντα δὲ δίψαισ᾽ ὑπὰ καύματος,   gl^{2c}//
— —— ‿ ‿— — ‿ ‿ — — ‿ ‿ — ‿ —//

At the end of a strophe, we find ph, hipp, or a finally compounded gl, or their acephalous forms. The uncompounded gl is not used as a clausula, which is only natural since it ends less heavily than the others. The blunt dactylic clausula . . . — ‿ ‿ —// is never found in Aeolic meters. The most typical clausula of a predominantly glyconic sequence is a pherecratean.

Example: Sophocles, *Oedipus Rex* 1201–1203:

ἐξ οὗ καὶ βασιλεὺς καλῇ   gl//
— — — ‿ ‿ — ‿ —//

ἐμὸς καὶ τὰ μέγιστ᾽ ἐτι-   gl
‿ — — ‿ ‿ — ‿-

μάθης, ταῖς μεγάλαισιν ἐν   gl
— — — ‿ ‿ — — ‿ —

Θήβαισιν ἀνάσσων.   ˄ph ///
— — ‿ ‿ — — ///

The Aeolic writers, notably Sappho and Alcaeus, generally apply much stricter standards of prosody than the non-Aeolic writers. Hiatus and elision are severely controlled, and mute plus liquid always lengthens the preceding syllable. But see above, section 2.

17. Pindar and Bacchylides

The strophic structures of Pindar and Bacchylides are more massive than those of their predecessors. Furthermore, while Sappho and Alcaeus and the other writers of monody compose their poems of single metrically uniform strophes following one after another: A///A///A///. . . . , choral poetry had by the time of Pindar and Bacchylides evolved a pattern in which two responding strophic units, called *strophe* and *antistrophe*, are followed by an *epode* (not to be confused with the other meaning of epode discussed in connection with the innovations of Archilochus, above, section 15). The whole *triad* is then repeated several times: A///A///B///A///A///B///A/// A///B///. . . .

The poems of Pindar and Bacchylides are composed of

(1) verses derived from iambic meters;
(2) Dactylo-epitrites;
(3) Dactylo-iambics;
(4) Aeolic meters.

Of these, (1) and (3) occur in only a few instances. Most of the poems which have come down to us may be characterized as Dactylo-epitritic or Aeolic.

1. *Verses derived from iambic meters.*

Example: Pindar, *Olympians* 2. 1–4:

'Αναξιφόρμιγγες ὕμνοι,
∪ — ∪ — — ∪ — — ||
τίνα θεόν, τίν' ἥρωα, τίνα δ' ἄνδρα κελαδήσομεν;
∪∪ ∪— ∪ —— ∪∪ — ∪ ∪∪— ∪ —||

ἤτοι Πίσα μὲν Διός· Ὀλυμπιάδα δ' ἔστασεν Ἡρακλέης
— ∪ — — ∪ ∪   ∪ — ∪ ∪ ∪   — — ∪ — — ∪ —//
ἀκρόθινα πολέμου·
— ∪ — ∪   ∪ ∪ — //

Another example: Bacchylides No. 17. 1–4:

Κυανόπρωρα μὲν ναῦς μενέκτυπον
∪ ∪ ∪ — ∪ —   —   ∪ — ∪ —

Θησέα δὶς ἑπτά τ' ἀγλαοὺς ἄγουσα
— ∪ ∪   ∪ — ∪   — ∪ — ∪ — ∪

κούρους Ἰαόνων
— — ∪ — ∪ —/

Κρητικὸν τάμνε πέλαγος·
— ∪ —   — ∪ ∪ ∪ — //

In both poems, the longa are combined in groups of one and two, the brevia in groups of one and three; ancipitia appear only at the beginning of a period. The sequence of elements resembles that in an iambic or cretic series, except that the periods do not contain complete metra; if one begins counting at the beginning, he is left with an excess at the end, and vice versa. It appears that the meters discussed in sections 15 and 16, and especially the technique of compounding, have affected the lyric iambs in such a manner as to relax their metrical regularity. The result is a free flow of iambic rhythm rather than a structure built up from recognizable units.

The two poems from which we have quoted are the only complete poems extant to exhibit this type of iambic verse. But cf. also Pindar frs. 105 and 108.

2. *Dactylo-epitrites.* In this meter, the basic groups *D* (— ∪ ∪ — ∪ ∪ —) and *e* (— ∪ —; cf. also the sigla at the end of section 1) are connected by means of an anceps which is usually long.* Ancipitia are used also to begin and to end a

* The form *e*×, i.e., usually, — ∪ — —, is known as the *epitrite*, so called because the first part of the group (— ∪) stands to the second (— —) in the relation 3 : 4.

35

period. The anceps between the basic groups is occasionally omitted, especially towards the end of the strophe.

The most common larger unit, $D \times e \times$, is identical in form with the encomiologicus (see above, section 15 near end), which appears in Simonides fr. 57 D. 3:

$$τᾶσδ' ἄτερ οὐδὲ θεῶν ζαλωτὸς αἰών.$$
$$— \; \cup\cup \; — \cup \; \cup — \; — \; — \cup \; — —//$$

Since Dactylo-epitrites, both in Pindar and Bacchylides and in drama, are used prominently in songs of praise, there is some justice in deriving the genre from this particular species of asynarteton.

e occasionally exhibits a resolved longum; in d or D resolution of a longum or substitution of a longum for two brevia is virtually unknown, as is the resolution of a connecting anceps.

Example of resolution in e: Pindar, *Olympians* 3. 10:

$$θεόμοροι νίσοντ' ἐπ' ἀνθρώπους ἀοιδαί, \qquad e—E—|||$$
$$\cup\cup\cup — \; — \; — \; \cup \; — \; — \; — \cup — —///$$

d^1 occurs principally in the combination: $e \times d^1 \, e$, i.e.,
$$— \cup — \times — \cup \cup — — \cup —(\times).$$

Example: Pindar, *Pythians* 1. 2:

$$σύνδικον Μοισᾶν κτέανον· τᾶς ἀκούει$$
$$— \cup — \; — \; — \; \cup\cup — \; — \; \cup — —$$

d^2 occurs chiefly after D: $— \cup\cup — \cup\cup — \cup\cup —$, or at the beginning of a strophe: $|||\cup \cup — —$ . . . .

Example of the latter: Pindar, *Olympians* 7. 1:

$$Φιάλαν ὡς εἴ τις ἀφνειᾶς ἀπὸ χειρὸς ἑλὼν \qquad d^2—e—D \, ||$$
$$\cup\cup \; — \; — — \cup \; — — \; — \cup\cup — \; \cup \; — \cup —//$$

A Dactylo-epitritic strophe usually ends in e: $— \cup — (\times)$; in tragedy the clausula is often ithyphallic. For an early lyric example of the ithyphallic ending we may cite Simonides fr. 48 D. 6:

καὶ βρότεοι παλάμαι θραύοντι· μωροῦ φωτὸς ἅδε βούλα.
— ◡ ◡— ◡ ◡ — — — ◡ — — — ◡ —◡ — —///

$$D-e-\text{ith} ///$$

Bacchylides' early Dactylo-epitritic poems are nearly as simple as those of Simonides, but under the influence of Pindar, who wrote more complex structures from the very beginning, Bacchylides also elaborated his scheme.

Here is an example of Bacchylides' early manner: No. 13. 58–66:

ἐκ τοῦ παρὰ βωμὸν ἀριστάρχου Διὸς $-D-e /$
— — ◡ ◡ — ◡ ◡ — — ◡ —/

Νίκας φερεκυδέος ἀνστεφθεῖσιν ἄνθεα $-D-e- /$
— — ◡◡ — ◡◡ — — ◡ —/

χρυσέαν δόξαν πολύφαντον ἐν αἰῶνι τρέφει παύροις
— ◡— — — ◡ ◡ — ◡ ◡ — — — ◡

βροτῶν $e-D-E //$
◡ — //

αἰεί, καὶ ὅταν θανάτοιο κυάνεον νέφος καλύψῃ, λείπεται
—— ◡ ◡ — ◡ ◡ —◡ — ◡ — ◡ — ◡ — — ◡—//

$$-D \cup e \cup e-e //$$

ἀθάνατον κλέος εὖ ἐρχθέντος ἀσφαλεῖ σὺν αἴσᾳ.
— ◡ ◡ — ◡ ◡ — — — ◡ — ◡ — ◡ — —///

$$D-e \cup e- ///$$

Note the steady alternation of D and E or e. There is a smoothness to this rhythm which Pindar usually avoids.

Example: Pythians 1. 1–4:

Χρυσέα φόρμιγξ, 'Απόλλωνος καὶ ἰοπλοκάμων $E-D //$
— ◡— — — ◡ ◡ — — ◡◡ — //

σύνδικον Μοισᾶν κτέανον· τᾶς ἀκούει $e-d^1 e-$
— ◡— — — ◡◡— — ◡——

μὲν βάσις ἀγλαΐας ἀρχά, $D-- //$
— ◡ ◡ — ◡◡— — —//

πείθονται δ' ἀοιδοὶ σάμασιν $--E //$
— — — ◡ — —◡ —//

ἀγησιχόρων ὁπόταν προοιμίων $-D \cup e$
— ◡◡ — ◡ ◡ — ◡ — —

ἀμβολὰς τεύχῃς ἐλελιζομένα. $e-D /$
— ◡ — — — ◡◡—◡ —/

37

But the difference between the rhythms of Pindar and those of Bacchylides is most apparent in the matter of word endings. Bacchylides avoids breaks after a connecting anceps, especially near the beginning and the end of the verse where these are in epitrite rhythm. When he does have a break after anceps, it seems that Bacchylides considers the grouping /—∪—×/ less attractive than the grouping /×—∪—×/ (compare the rhythm of the iambic trimeter, above, section 7). Pindar, on the other hand, cannot be said to observe any rule concerning breaks. Perhaps he found that Bacchylides' practice made for added monotony in a meter which in unskilled hands might create a monotonous effect in any case. What is more, Pindar commits some real infractions of the strict rules of metrics, including that of breaking up metrical units by means of pauses.

Example: Olympians 6. 5–6:

$$\Delta\iota\grave{o}s \; \grave{\epsilon}\nu \; \Pi\acute{\iota}\sigma\alpha, \; \sigma\upsilon\nu\sigma\iota\kappa\iota\sigma\tau\acute{\eta}\rho \; \tau\epsilon$$
∪ ∪ — ∪ —́ // ∪ — — —́ ∪

where —//∪— cannot be anything but *e*. But even in Pindar the majority of the bridges occur between anceps and following element.

3. *Dactylo-iambics.* Dactylic and epitritic units may be combined in a manner which produces an iambic effect. For instance, in Bacchylides No. 19 the anceps which joins *e*-units to *D*- and *d¹*-units is short throughout. Bacchylides' opening words suggest that this poem is in the nature of an experiment:

$$\Pi\acute{\alpha}\rho\epsilon\sigma\tau\iota \; \mu\upsilon\rho\acute{\iota}\alpha \; \kappa\acute{\epsilon}\lambda\epsilon\upsilon\theta\sigma s \; \grave{\alpha}\mu\beta\rho\sigma\sigma\acute{\iota}\omega\nu \; \mu\epsilon\lambda\acute{\epsilon}\omega\nu, \qquad \cup E \cup / D /$$
∪ — ∪ — ∪— ∪ — ∪ / — ∪ ∪ — ∪∪ —/

$$\grave{o}s \; \grave{\alpha}\nu \; \pi\alpha\rho\grave{\alpha} \; \Pi\iota\epsilon\rho\acute{\iota}\delta\omega\nu \; \lambda\acute{\alpha}\chi\eta\sigma\iota \; \delta\hat{\omega}\rho\alpha \; \text{Moυσ}\hat{\alpha}\nu,$$
∪ — ∪ ∪ —∪∪ — ∪ —∪ — ∪ — —//
$$\cup D \cup \text{ith} //$$

38

4. *Aeolic meters.* Bacchylides' Aeolic poems, as well as some of the simpler poems in that genre written by Pindar, employ the forms sketched above, section 16.

Example: Bacchylides No. 18. 1–7:

Βασιλεῦ τᾶν ἱερᾶν 'Αθανᾶν, τῶν ἀβροβίων ἄναξ 'Ιώνων,
ᴗ ᴗ — — ᴗᴗ— ᴗ — — / — — ᴗᴗ — ᴗ — ᴗ— —//
                                                        hipp/ₐgl ba//

τί νέον ἔκλαγε χαλκοκώδων σάλπιγξ πολεμηΐαν ἀοιδάν;
ᴗ ᴗᴗ — ᴗᴗ — ᴗ — — — — — ᴗ ᴗ—ᴗ— ᴗ— — //
                                                        hipp ₐgl ba//

ἦ τις ἀμετέρας χθονὸς δυσμενὴς ὅρι' ἀμφιβάλ-   2 gl
— ᴗ — ᴗᴗ — ᴗ — — ᴗ — ᴗᴗ — ᴗ —

λει στραταγέτας ἀνήρ;   lec/
— ᴗ — ᴗ — ᴗ —/

The poem continues in the same vein. The corresponding lines of the subsequent strophes clearly mark the location of the Aeolic bases by occasionally substituting a long for a short or a short for a long. Note that the base may exhibit resolution.

In most of his Aeolic poems, however, Pindar ventures much farther afield than this. The large majority of those of his poems not written in Dactylo-epitrites may be termed Aeolic because the first period in each case follows the rules observed by the Lesbians; it is in the sequel that Pindar develops his own variations.

These variations consist of the addition, omission, or repetition of certain elements, and of the transition to other unit sequences. The variety is so rich that it cannot be described in terms of rules. Each poem needs to be interpreted in its own right. A close analysis of the patterns will show that Pindar's periods are not clearly definable and autonomous units, but rather that each period can be understood only through the context in which it appears. We continue to denote periods by means of the sigla we have used in the previous sections, with the understanding that the notation

THE METERS OF GREEK AND LATIN POETRY

is approximate rather than definitive. For one thing, our ignorance of the musical tradition militates against setting up hard-and-fast schemes. In all of Pindar's poetry, it is the strophe rather than the period which counts as the complete unit. And that, we may add, is one of the characteristic differences between classical and archaic poetry.

Example: Pindar, *Olympians* 1. 1–11, 23–29:

Strophe

1 Ἄριστον μὲν ὕδωρ, ὁ δὲ
   ‿ − − ‿ − − ‿ −

        χρυσὸς αἰθόμενον πῦρ   gl ph//
        − ‿ − ‿ ‿ − − //

2 ἅτε διαπρέπει
   ‿ ‿ ‿ − ‿ −

        νυκτὶ μεγάνορος ἔξοχα πλούτου·   cr ph²ᵈ//
        − ‿ ‿ − ‿ ‿ − ‿ ‿ − − //

3 εἰ δ' ἄεθλα γαρύεν   cr ia//
   − ‿ − ‿ − ‿ − //

4   ἔλδεαι, φίλον ἦτορ,   ph//
            − ‿ − ‿ ‿ − − //

5 μηκέτ' ἀελίου σκόπει   cr ia//
   − ‿ − ‿ − ‿ − //

6 ἄλλο θαλπνότερον ἐν ἀμέρᾳ φαεννὸν
   − ‿ − ‿ ‿ ‿ ‿ − ‿ − ‿ ‿

        ἄστρον ἐρήμας δι' αἰθέρος,   cr 2 ia ₍ph ia//
        − ‿ ‿ − ‿ − ‿ − //

7 μηδ' Ὀλυμπίας ἀγῶ-
   − ‿ − ‿ − ‿

        να φέρτερον αὐδάσομεν·   cr ia ₍ph ‿ −//
        ‿ − ‿ ‿ − ‿ − //

8 ὅθεν ὁ πολύφατος ὕμνος ἀμφιβάλλεται   3 ia//
   ‿ ‿ ‿ ‿ ‿ ‿ − ‿ ‿ − ‿ −//

9 σοφῶν μητίεσσι, κελαδεῖν   ‿ − 2 cr//
   ‿ − − ‿ − ‿ ‿ ‿ − //

10 Κρόνου παῖδ' ἐς ἀφνεὰν ἱκομένους   ba ia cr//
   ‿ − − − ‿ − ‿ ‿ ‿ − //

11 μάκαιραν Ἱέρωνος ἑστίαν,   ia cr ‿ −///
   ‿ − ‿ ‿ ‿ − ‿ − ‿ −///

40

Epode

1 Συρακόσιον ἱπποχάρμαν βασιλῆα·
    ‿ — ‿‿‿ — ‿ — ‿‿‿—‿

                λάμπει δέ οἱ κλέος   ia cr cho ba ia//
                — — ‿ — ‿ —//

2 ἐν εὐάνορι Λυδοῦ Πέλοπος ἀποικία·   ‿ — cho cr ia//
    ‿ — ‿‿ — — ‿ ‿‿ ‿—‿—//

3 τοῦ μεγασθενὴς ἐράσσατο Γαιάοχος   tr — ‿ cho cr//
    — ‿ — ‿ — ‿— ‿‿ —‿—//

4 Ποσειδάν, ἐπεί νιν καθαροῦ λέβητος
    ‿ — — ‿ — — ‿‿ — ‿ — ‿

                ἔξελε Κλωθώ,   ba gl ₗph//
                — ‿‿ — —//

5 ἐλέφαντι   φαίδιμον ὤ-
    ‿‿ — ‿   — ‿‿ —

                μον κεκαδμένον.   polysch —‿ — ‿—//
                — ‿ — ‿ —//

6 ἦ θαύματα πολλά, καί πού τι
    — — ‿‿ — ‿ — — ‿

                καὶ βροτῶν   ₗgl — ‿ — ‿ —//
                — ‿ —//

7 φάτις ὑπὲρ τὸν ἀλαθῆ λόγον   ‿ ‿‿ cho cr//
    ‿ ‿ ‿ — — ‿—‿ //

8 δεδαιδαλμένοι ψεύδεσι ποικίλοις
    ‿ — — ‿ — — ‿‿ — ‿ —

                ἐξαπατῶντι μῦθοι.   ba gl cho ba///
                — ‿‿ — ‿ — —///

The poem begins with a regular Aeolic sequence of gl ph//, also known as priapean. The second period compounds the ph internally with two dactyls, prefixing to the whole unit the three elements which immediately precede the ph of the first period, with one longum resolved. The elements also happen to be metrically equivalent to the initial bacchiac of the first period. By another analysis, the second period is almost identical with the first, except that the elements — ‿ ‿ of the gl have been placed after the following three elements, and that the base of the ph has been extended from — ‿ to — ‿ ‿. The third period extends the beginning of the second to a dimeter, different from gl only in that there is only one

breve instead of the "choriambic" two. The fourth period
once more exhibits the ph of the first. The fifth repeats the
third; the sixth extends this dimeter to a trimeter and
appends to it an acephalous ph and a further iambic metron.
The seventh period abbreviates the preceding by one metron
at the beginning, and by half a metron at the end. The eighth
takes up the trimeter of the sixth, but starts it off with a full ia
rather than cr. The ninth reduces these three metra, the first
to half an ia, the other two to cr. The tenth extends the pre-
ceding by $-\smile$, which results in the sequence ba ia cr, the first
two of which resemble the gl of the first period, except that
they are shorter by one breve. The eleventh varies the tenth
by completing the first metron and abbreviating the second
and third; an alternative formulation would be to say that it
differs from the preceding only in that the first (resolved)
longum of the final cr has been omitted.

The epode repeats the beginning of the last period of the
strophe but develops it in the form of the gl of the first period
of the strophe. But whereas the original gl was followed by a
ph, it is here succeeded by the last few elements of the final
period of the strophe: $-\smile-\smile-$. Thus we have a pentameter
of predominantly iambic character whose middle metron is
choriambic. The second period resembles the first, except
that the first six elements are dropped and that a kind of
anaclasis has changed the last but one metron from ba to cr.
Hence the beginning is equal to ph, reminding us of the
second half of the first period of the strophe (an effect en-
hanced by the break after the ph). The third period differs
from the second in eliminating the final ia and adding an
initial tro; consequently the base of the ph is $-\smile$ rather than
$\smile-$. In other words, the ph is preceded by a duplication of
its first four elements. In the fourth period, gl and ph are
once more joined, as in the first period of the strophe, but the

ph is acephalous, and the gl is preceded by ba (duplication of the first three elements of gl). In the fifth period, ph is followed by ia as in the sixth period of the strophe, but the metron which stood at the beginning of the third and fourth periods is further reduced to the form of two brevia, with the result that the period resembles a polyschematist with an added $-\smile-\smile-$. In the sixth period we have an acephalous gl followed by the same tro. The seventh period is an abbreviation of the fifth, and the eighth approximates the fourth, with this difference that for clausula it has cho ba rather than acephalous ph.

It should once more be stressed that our analysis is by no means the only one possible. The student will perhaps be repelled by an analysis which is both tentative and unwieldy. If he asks what light such counting of elements will throw on the aesthetic character of the poem, no quick answer can be given (for an attempt to supply an answer in the case of a less complicated structure, see below, *Appendix*). But it is obvious that we cannot begin to define the special nature of each poem and of individual lines in the poem until we determine the metrical genre of the poem as a whole in relation to the genres available to Pindar when he began writing, and until we study the kinship between the various periods of the poem. Our sample analysis does not make for ready conclusions, but it helps to assemble some of the raw materials required for an exhaustive interpretation of the work.

18. Tragedy and Comedy

While non-dramatic choral lyrics usually are triadic (cf. above, section 17), in drama strophe and antistrophe are used only once, to be followed by another combination of strophe and antistrophe, and so forth: A///A///B///B///C/// C///. . . . After an antistrophe or at the end of the whole ode we sometimes find a non-responding *astrophon* called *epode* (contrast the responding epode, above, section 17, and the Archilochean epode, above, section 15). Similarly an astrophon is occasionally found *between* strophe and antistrophe, in which case it is called a *mesode* (*Example:* Aeschylus, *Choephori* 789–793), or even *before* the strophe, in which case it is called a *proode* (*Example:* Aristophanes, *Acharnians* 1143–1149).

Here is an example of an antistrophe followed by an epode: Aeschylus, *Prometheus Bound* 894–906:

Antistrophe

μήποτε μήποτέ μ', ὦ   *D*/
— ∪ ∪ — ∪ ∪ — /

Μοῖραι ⟨μακραίωνες⟩, λεχέων Διὸς εὐνά-   — *e* — *D* —
— — — ∪ — ∪ ∪— ∪ ∪ — —

τειραν ἴδοισθε πέλουσαν·   *D* —//
— ∪ ∪ — ∪ ∪ — —//

μηδὲ πλαθείην γαμέτᾳ τινὶ τῶν ἐξ οὐρανοῦ.   *e* — *D* — *e*//
—∪ — — ∪ ∪— ∪ ∪ — — — ∪ —//

ταρβῶ γὰρ ἀστεργάνορα παρθενίαν   — *e* — *D*//
— — ∪ — — ∪ ∪ — ∪ ∪—//

εἰσορῶσ' Ἰοῦς ἀμαλαπτομέναν   *e* —*D*//
—∪ — — — ∪ ∪— ∪ ∪ — //

δυσπλάνοις Ἥρας ἀλατείαις πόνων.   *E* — *e*///
— ∪ — — — ∪ — — — ∪ — ///

Epode

ἐμοὶ δ' ὅτε μὲν ὁμαλὸς ὁ γάμος,   2 ia(?)
∪ — ∪ ∪ ∪ ∪ ∪ ∪ ∪ ∪

ἄφοβος· ὃν δὲ δέδια, μὴ   tro cr
∪ ∪ ∪ — ∪ ∪∪∪ —

κρεισσόνων ἔρως ἄφυκτον ὄμμα προσδράκοι με.   2 tro ith//
— ∪ — ∪ — ∪— ∪ —∪ — ∪ — —//

ἀπόλεμος ὅδε γ' ὁ πόλεμος, ἄπορα πόριμος· οὐδ'   3 ia
∪ ∪∪ ∪ ∪ ∪∪ ∪ ∪ ∪ ∪ ∪ ∪ ∪ ∪ ∪ ∪ —

ἔχω τίς ἂν γενοίμαν·   ia ba//
∪— ∪ — ∪— — //

44

τὰν Διὸς γὰρ οὐχ ὁρῶ   tro cr/
 — ∪ — ∪ — — /

μῆτιν ὄπα φύγοιμ' ἄν.   cho ba///
 — ∪ ∪ — ∪ — — ///

The antistrophe is written in simple Dactylo-epitrites, of the
kind used by Stesichorus and Simonides. Its periods are short
and clearly defined. The epode, with its prevailing iambo-
trochaic rhythm, its wealth of resolution, and its paucity of
clear-cut pauses, is in striking contrast to the rhythm of
strophe and antistrophe.

While there are dramatic odes whose strophes are com-
posed of units belonging to one and the same meter, as the
Aeschylean antistrophe quoted above, most of them change
meter within the strophe. The dramatists are not the first to
mix meters within the strophe. An early example of this pro-
cedure is found in Alcman's *Partheneion* col. ii lines 11–15
Page:

οὐδ' ἁμῶς ἐῇ· δοκεῖ γὰρ ἤμεν αὔτα   3 tro//
— ∪ — ∪— ∪ — — ∪ — — //

ἐκπρεπὴς τὼς ὥπερ αἴ τις   2 tro/
— ∪ — — — ∪ — /

ἐν βοτοῖς στάσειεν ἵππον   4 tro//
— ∪ — — — ∪ — — //

παγὸν ἀεθλοφόρον καναχάποδα   4 da/
— ∪ ∪— ∪ ∪ — ∪ ∪ — ∪ ∪ /

τῶν ὑποπετριδίων ὀνείρων.   4 da ∪⁀ — — ///
— ∪ ∪ — ∪ ∪ — ∪ — — ///

Perhaps it is not without significance that this early
example of mixed trochees and dactyls occurs in a poem
which was written for delivery by two contending choruses,
i.e., for a dramatic performance of a sort. Metrical hetero-
geneity, then, may well be a hallmark of dramatic lyric
poetry. Alcman's procedure is comparatively simple; he
combines his meters by juxtaposing autonomous units and
periods. As the notation above shows, it is on the whole easy
to isolate the components of which the system is made up.

A rather similar situation is found in Attic comedy. In most of Aristophanes' lyric odes the technique is roughly the same as in the *Partheneion.*

Example: Aristophanes, *Frogs* 449–454:

χωρῶμεν ἐς πολυρρόδους	2 ia/
— ‿ — ‿ — ‿ — /	
λειμῶνας ἀνθεμώδεις,	ia ba//
— — ‿ — ‿ — — //	
τὸν ἡμέτερον τρόπον	₋gl/
‿ — ‿‿— ‿ — /	
τὸν καλλιχορώτατον	₋gl/
— — ‿‿ — ‿ — /	
παίζοντες, ὃν ὄλβιαι	₋gl/
— — ‿ ‿ — ‿ — /	
Μοῖραι ξυνάγουσιν.	₋ph///
— — ‿‿ — — — ///	

The transition from iambic to Aeolic rhythm is of course easily brought about. Indeed, the combination has a precedent in the externally compounded Aeolic meters of Sappho and Alcaeus (cf. above, section 16).

The lyric of tragedy, on the other hand, usually combines the units of various meters in such a manner that they lose their original identity and make for a larger organic whole, a whole which can no longer easily be associated with this or that particular meter. The means whereby this freer composition is achieved may be termed the *sliding transition.**

The most obvious case of a sliding transition is the change from one meter to another via a unit which is ambivalent, i.e., which may be regarded as belonging either to the first or the second meter. Thus in the following example the

* Bacchylides changes meters only once, and then between antistrophe and epode; his third poem has an Iambo–Aeolic strophe and a Dactylo-epitritic epode (compare the similar case of Aeschylus, *Prometheus Bound* 894–906, quoted above). Pindar's *Olympians* 13 which has transition within the strophe is probably influenced by the Attic dramatists.

transition from a dactylic to an Aeolic unit is obtained via a
pherecratean with two longa in the base:

$$-\cup\cup-\cup\cup-- \qquad\qquad 3\ da_\wedge$$
$$---\cup\cup-- \qquad\qquad 3\ da_\wedge = ph$$
$$---\cup\cup-\cup- \qquad\qquad gl$$

But the ambivalent unit is not the only means of achieving
a sliding transition. It may also result from a slight variation
of the original elements, or from a different distribution of
word endings which will approximate one meter to another
An example of the last will be found in Aeschylus, *Persians*
647–651:

ἦ φίλος ἀνήρ, φίλος ὄχθος· φίλα γὰρ κέκευθεν ἤθη.
$-\ \cup\cup\ -\stackrel{}{-}_{/}\ \cup\cup\ \stackrel{}{-}-_{/}\ \cup\cup\ -\ \cup\ -\ \cup\ \stackrel{}{-}-_{//}$

'Αιδωνεὺς δ' ἀναπομπὸς   ἀνίει,
$\cup\cup\ -\ -\ _{/}\ \ \cup\cup\ -\ \cup\qquad \cup--_{//}$

'Αιδωνεύς, οἷον ἀνάκτορα Δαριᾶνα.
$\cup\cup\ -\ -\ _{/}-\cup\ \cup\ -\ \cup\cup\ \ -\cup--_{///}$

The first period seems to begin with 3 cho, but the word
endings (here further marked by punctuation) suggest ionics,
and the second half of the period actually turns out to be an
anaclast. Hence the first five elements of the line are better
regarded as non-choriambic, perhaps dactylic. The second
period continues with ionics, but the truncating of the second
metron creates a transition to dactylic rhythm. The third
period once more starts out with ionics (connecting with the
second period also by *anaphora*, that is to say, the words be-
ginning the lines are identical), but then slides into pure
dactyls, with the clausula of the strophe once more mirroring
the end of the first period. Hence we may now conclude that
the first five elements of the first period should also be
analyzed as dactyls.

To document the principle of the sliding transition, it will

be useful to analyze three further passages from Attic drama.
First, Aeschylus, *Suppliants* 40–48:

1	νῦν δ' ἐπικεκλομένα — ‿‿— ‿ ‿—∕	3 da$_{\wedge\wedge}$∕
2	Δῖον πόρτιν ὑπερπόντιον τι- — — — ‿ ‿ — —‿— —	3 da$_{\wedge\wedge}$ tro = ph ba
3	μάορ' ἴνιν τ' ἀνθονόμον — ‿ — — — ‿ ‿ —∕	tro cho∕
4	τᾶς προγόνου βοὸς ἐξ ἐπιπνοίας — ‿‿ — ‿‿ — ‿‿——∕	4 da$_{\wedge}$∕
5	Ζηνός· ἔφαψιν ἐπωνυμίᾳ δ' ἐπε- — ‿ ‿ —‿ ‿—‿‿— ‿ ‿	4 da
6	κραίνετο μόρσιμος αἰὼν — ‿‿ — ‿‿ — —∕	3 da$_{\wedge}$∕
7	εὐλόγως, Ἔπαφόν τ' ἐγέννασεν· — ‿ — ‿ ‿— ‿— — —∕∕∕	gl— —∕∕∕

The strophe begins with a hemiepes. In the second line the
hemiepes is repeated, but with a dissyllabic first dactyl.
The elements after the first dactyl of the second line may also
by analyzed as a choriamb. But if we add the following
trochee, the whole may finally be regarded as a combination
of pherecratean and bacchiac. Dactyls, trochees, choriambs
and Aeolic: these are the meters which continue to be opera-
tive in the rest of the strophe, and indeed throughout this
first stasimon of the play. The ending of line 3 is choriambic.
The breaks at the beginning of line 4 seem to suggest that the
choriambic rhythm is continued, but the line turns out to be
dactylic, like the first. Finally, the seventh line diverges from
the fourth by omitting a breve from the first dactyl and
lengthening a breve towards the end, with the result that the
seventh line comes to resemble the second.

Second example: Sophocles, *Antigone* 604–614 (lines 3 and 4
emended):

1	τεάν, Ζεῦ, δύνασιν τίς ἀνδρῶν ‿— — ‿‿ — ‿ — — ∕	hipp∕
2	ὑπερβασία κατάσχοι; ‿ —‿‿— ‿ — —∕∕	$_{\wedge}$hipp∕∕

3 τὰν οὔθ᾽ ὕπνος αἱρεῖ ποθ᾽ ὁ πάντ᾽ ἀγρεύων, ₐhippᶜ//
   — — ◡ ◡ — — ◡ ◡ — ◡ — — //

4   οὔτε θεῶν ἄκματοι   cho ba/
            — ◡ ◡ — — ◡ — /

5 μῆνες, ἀγήρως δὲ χρόνῳ δυνάστας   2 cho ba//
  — ◡ ◡— — ◡ ◡ — ◡ — — //

6   κατέχεις ᾽Ολύμπου   anclₐₐ/
           ◡ ◡ — ◡ — — /

7   μαρμαρόεσσαν αἴγλαν.   cho ba//
         — ◡ ◡— ◡ — — //

8   τό τ᾽ ἔπειτα καὶ τὸ μέλλον   anacl/
      ◡ ◡ — ◡ — ◡ — — /

9 καὶ τὸ πρὶν ἐπαρκέσει   ₐgl/
  — — ◡ ◡ — ◡ — /

10   νόμος ὅδ᾽· οὐδὲν ἕρπει   cr ba//
         ◡ ◡ ◡ — ◡ — — //

11 θνατῶν βιότῳ   πάμπολύ γ᾽ ἐκτὸς ἄτας. ₐhippᶜ///
  — — ◡◡—   — ◡◡ — ◡ — — ///

Line 4 is a repetition of line 2 except that the first element is missing; line 6 stands in the same relationship to line 4. Lines 3 and 5 repeat lines 2 and 4, with the addition of a choriamb. Line 7 is identical with line 4, line 11 with line 3. Line 9 is a variant of line 7; line 10 is intermediate between lines 6 and 7. Again, it is more important to appreciate the formal variations and the basic relationships than to recognize the standard elements.

Third example: Euripides, *Medea* 131–138:

1 ἔκλυον φωνάν, ἔκλυον δὲ βοὰν   2 an//
  ◡◡ — — — / ◡◡ — ◡ ◡ — //

2 τᾶς δυστάνου Κολχίδος, οὐδέ πω   2 an/
  — — — — / — ◡ ◡ ◡ — ◡ ◡ /

3 ἤπιος: ἀλλ᾽ ὦ γηραιά,   2 anₐ// = 4 daₐₐ//
  —◡◡ — — — — //

4 λέξον· ἐπ᾽ ἀμφιπύλου γὰρ ἔσω μελάθρου βοὰν 5 da◡ —//
  — ◡ ◡ ◡ — ◡ ◡ ◡ — ◡ ◡ — ◡ ◡ — ◡ — //

5 ἔκλυον· οὐδὲ συνήδομαι, ὦ γύναι, ἄλγεσιν 5 da◡ —//
  — ◡◡ ◡ ◡ — ◡ ◡ — ◡ ◡ — ◡ — //

6 δώματος. ἐπεί μοι φίλον κέκρανται.   ia cr ba///
  — ◡ ◡ ◡ — — ◡ — ◡ — — ///

Anapaests here turn into dactyls, and the dactylic clausula prepares the iambic ending of the strophe.

19. Dochmiacs

The dochmiac is a new creation of tragedy. Its forms are greatly variable, but the basic form is the sequence ×−−∪−, two of which naturally combine to make up a dimeter.

Example: Sophocles, *Antigone* 1317–1318:

ὤμοι μοι, τάδ' οὐκ ἐπ' ἄλλον βροτῶν   2 doch/
− − − ∪ − ∪ − ∪ − /

ἐμᾶς ἁρμόσει ποτ' ἐξ αἰτίας.   2 doch/
∪ − − ∪ − ∪ − − ∪ − /

But in most cases the metrical scheme is less regular. Longa are resolved, a breve may reduplicate itself, and dochmiac units are interspersed with straight or truncated iambs to form compound periods of which it is not always possible to say whether they are to be termed iambic or dochmiac.

Example: Aeschylus, *Agamemnon* 1173–1177:

1	ἑπόμενα προτέροισι τάδ' ἐφημίσω. ∪ ∪ ∪ ∪ ∪ ∪ − ∪ ∪ ∪ − ∪ − //	2 doch//
2	καί τίς σε κακοφρονῶν τίθη- − − ∪ ∪ ∪ ∪ − ∪ −	2 ia
3	σι δαίμων ὑπερβαρὴς ἐμπίτνων ∪ − − ∪ − ∪ − ∪ − /	2 doch/
4	μελίζειν πάθη γοερὰ θανατοφόρα. ∪ − − ∪ − ∪ ∪ ∪ ∪ ∪ ∪ ∪ ∪ /	2 doch/
5	τέρμα δ' ἀμηχανῶ. − ∪ ∪ − ∪ − ///	doch///

Line 2 consists of an iambic dimeter, with the second longum of the first metron resolved. But the absence of a break at its end indicates that it forms one unit with the regular dochmiac dimeter which follows. The dochmiacs which surround this unit, i.e., lines 1, 4 and 5, exhibit the

50

metron in various stages of resolution. On the basis of this passage alone, we would have to allow for the following scheme:

$$\overset{\cup\cup}{\underset{\cup}{\smile}} \ \underset{\cup\cup}{\smile} \ \underset{\cup\cup}{\smile} \ _\times \ \underset{\cup}{\smile}.$$

Substitution of double breve for the short fourth element of the basic form is also found.

The staccato rhythm of dochmiacs makes them suitable for the expression of violent emotions, especially fear and despair. Here then we have one lyric meter which, unlike most of the others discussed, can be associated with a particular mood or sentiment. Though similar associations can occasionally be suggested for other meters (cf. the remarks about the use of lyric dactyls, above, section 10), the dochmiac is the only lyric meter of which it can be said that it is calculated to evoke a specific emotional response.

20. Post-Classical Developments

After the classical age there were no radically new ventures in metrical matters. The traditional meters were, however, developed in several opposite directions.

1. Hellenistic writers began to use some of the older lyric meters, particularly Aeolic meters, in stichic sequence (cf. above, section 9), to be recited rather than sung. The so-called *asclepiadean*, for instance (notation: gl^c; see above, section 16), a unit not unknown to Alcaeus, is named after the Hellenistic poet Asclepiades who presumably composed long passages consisting entirely of periods of this type. Other less common names for certain groups of elements were similarly derived from Hellenistic writers using such groups in stichic sequence. For the names, see the *Glossary*.

2. The so-called *dithyramb*, a semi-dramatic literary form of the fifth century B.C., was developed further in the direction

51

of complete freedom from responsion and from traditional metrical units. Our chief example of this type of writing is Timotheus' *Persians* in which there are long passages of iambs, with transitions to trochees and dactyls, and occasional dochmiacs, polyschematists and glyconics; the verse adapts itself to the quickly changing pace of the dramatic action.

Example: col. v, lines 191–209 Wilamowitz:

Ἰὼ κατασκαφαὶ δόμων ∪— ∪ — ∪ — ∪ —	2 ia
σείριαί τε νᾶες Ἑλλανίδες. — ∪— ∪ —∪ — — ∪ —//	tro 2 cr//
αἳ κατὰ μὲν ἤλικ' ὀλέσαθ' ἤ- — ∪∪ ∪ — ∪ ∪∪∪ —	2 ia
βαν νέων πολύανδρον, — ∪— ∪∪— — /	ph/
νᾶες δὲ — — —	— — —
οὐκ ὀπισσοπόρευτον ἄ- — ∪— ∪∪ — ∪ —	gl
ξουσιν, πυρὸς δ' αἰθαλόεν — — ∪— '— ∪ ∪—/	ia cho/
μένος ἀγρίῳ σώματι φλέ- ∪∪ ∪∪— — ∪∪ —	2 cho
ξει, στονόεντα δ' ἄλγη — ∪ ∪—∪ — — //	cho ba = 3 da ∪ — — // ʌʌ
ἔσται Περσίδι χώρᾳ. — — — ∪∪ — — //	ph = 3 daʌ//
ὢ βαρεῖα συμφορά, — ∪— ∪ — ∪ —//	tro cr//
ἅ μ' ἐς Ἑλλάδ' ἤγαγες. — ∪ — ∪ — ∪ —//	tro cr//
ἀλλ' ἴτε μηκέτι μέλλετε ζεύγνυτε — ∪∪ — ∪∪ — ∪∪ — ∪ ∪	4 da/
μὲν τετράορον ἵππων — ∪— ∪∪ — —//	ph//
ὄχημ', οἳ δ' ἀνάριθμον ὀλ- ∪— ∪ — ∪∪— ∪ —	gl
βον φορεῖτ' ἐπ' ἀπήνας, — ∪— ∪ — ∪— —//	ph//
πίμπρατε δὲ σκηνάς, — ∪∪ — — —/	3 daʌʌ/

52

μηδέ τις ἡμετέρου   3 da/
‒ ◡ ◡ ‒ ◡ ◡ ‒ /

γένοιτ' ὄνησις αὐτοῖσι πλούτου.   ia 2 ba//
◡ ‒ ◡ ‒ ◡ ‒ ‒ ◡ ‒ ‒ //

It is obvious that the sigla appended in the margin cannot be proposed as reliable definitions of the metrical patterns of this aria. Once responsion has been abolished it is almost impossible to be sure about the meters which have gone into this sort of free verse. One cannot even be sure that the writer meant to make use of the metrical traditions and the basic patterns which the archaic age had evolved.

3. In the end, the Byzantine poets remodelled metrical usage to conform with the change from pitch accent to stress accent, and also to accommodate the new isochrony of vowel quantities, i.e., the new pronunciation in which all vowels, no matter what their original quantities, were allowed the same length of time in the conception of the verse. In the following sailors' shanty of the second century after Christ (J. U. Powell, ed., *Collectanea Alexandrina* (Oxford 1925), "Lyrica Adespota", 32) each line seems to carry three stresses, two of them generated by the rising rhythm of anapaests, and the third prompted by the uniformly paroxytone ending. Thus this poem represents an intermediate stage between rhythmic and accentual articulation.

Ναῦται βυθοκυματοδρόμοι
‒ ‒ ◡ ◡ ‒ ◡ ◡ ◡ ‒ /

ἁλίων Τρίτωνες ὑδάτων,
◡ ◡ ‒ ‒ ‒ ◡ ◡ ◡ ‒ /

καὶ Νειλῶται γλυκυδρόμοι
‒ ‒ ‒ ‒ ◡ ◡ ◡ ‒ /

τὰ γελῶντα πλέοντες ὑδάτη,
◡ ◡ ‒ ◡ ‒ ◡ ‒ ◡ ◡ ‒ /

τὴν σύγκρισιν εἴπατε, φίλοι,
‒ ‒ ◡ ◡ ◡ ‒ ◡ ◡ ◡ ‒ /

πελάγους καὶ Νείλου γονίμου.
◡ ◡ ‒ ‒ ‒ ‒ ◡ ◡ ‒ //

53

Compare also the choliambs of Babrius who ends each line with a paroxytone word. Similarly, in the hexameters of Nonnus proparoxytone ending is entirely ruled out.

21. Appendix

It should always be remembered that metrical analysis is merely one approach to the understanding of a poem. But to indicate the share which the metrical arrangement may have in the total effect produced by the poem, let us take a parting look at one brief specimen of verse: Archilochus fr. 16 D.:

$$\text{῾Υψηλοὺς Μεγάτιμον 'Αριστοφόωντά τε Νάξου}$$
$$- - - / \; \cup \cup - \cup / \; \cup - \cup \cup - \cup \cup / - - //$$
$$\text{κίονας, ὦ μεγάλη γαῖ', ὑπένερθεν ἔχεις.}$$
$$- \cup \cup - \cup \cup - / - \cup \cup - \cup \; \cup - ///$$

The couplet, a funerary inscription in the traditional elegiac meter, begins with a word meaning "high-towering" and ends with a phrase meaning "contain beneath". Apparently, then, the mental eye of the listener is guided from high to low. Metrically speaking, it will be noticed that the first line is full of heavy words, including one of seven syllables (counting word clusters), whereas the sequence of the second line is considerably more broken up. In the first line, the dislocation of the third caesura (cf. above, section 5) makes for a forward momentum; the heaviness of the parts is sustained by the scarcely interrupted progress of the whole. The second line has the usual diaeresis dividing it in the middle; nevertheless the rhythm of the line is jagged. Note the punctuation which sets off the address to Earth, and especially the comma after γαῖ', which serves in part to counteract and obscure the effect of the diaeresis. It appears, therefore, that the dynamic flow of the couplet, with its ponderous beginning and its harsher termination, has a life of its own. The nervous twist of the second line coming upon the solid march of the hexameter, seems to run counter to the spirit of the thought, to the expectation roused by the key-words "above" and "below". The clue lies in the words with which the two lines begin. The image of high columns being held or constrained underground, of vigorous soldiers being imprisoned in the lifeless dark, is underscored by the mechanics of the poem.

The Meters of Latin Poetry

The Meters of Latin Poetry

Introduction

With the exception of the Saturnian meter (see *Note* below), all meters of classical Latin poetry are based on Greek prototypes. Greek verse is quantitative, i.e., poetic rhythm is determined by a sequence of long and short elements and not, as in English, by the natural word accent. The Latin language, in its classical period at least, seems to have had a stress accent which followed the so-called "Penultimate Law", i.e., if the next-to-last syllable of a word is long, it carries the accent; if it is short, the accent falls on the syllable preceding it. As we shall see below, it may well be that this natural word stress alone carried the rhythm of the only indigenous Italic meter that we know, the Saturnian.

Exactly how a language with such an accent was able to base its poetry on the meters of a totally different kind of language is one of the most vexed questions of classical philology, which the scope of this book does not permit us to discuss in detail. That Latin poetry *did* model its verse structures on Greek meters is certain, and it seems that in doing so Latin found no such difficulties as English does, for example, when it tries to imitate the Greek (or Latin) hexameter. But at the same time, there can be no doubt that the natural word accent played some part in Latin poetry; not only do the rules governing *brevis brevians* (see below, section II. 4) remain incomprehensible without a consideration of word accent, but, as we shall see below, there is a coincidence of word accent and long element in certain word groups

59

within several metrical schemes. Some of this can no doubt be explained by reference to the Penultimate Law, which makes word accent on a long penultimate mandatory; it is, on the other hand, unlikely that the Roman poets should have ignored entirely the incidence of natural word accent on long elements in composing their verses.

Still, since the crucial fact about Latin verse is that it is quantitative, we shall, in the following pages, largely disregard word accent, and concentrate instead on the sequences of long and short syllables of which it is composed.

Note on the Saturnian

Although only about 160 lines of Saturnian verse have come down to us, the structure of no other Latin verse form has been more controversial. The only uncontested facts are (*a*) that it is the oldest Latin verse form of which we know, and (*b*) that we find it in early funerary inscriptions and in literary fragments, e.g., the *Sententiae* of Appius Claudius Caecus (censor in 312 B.C.), the translation of the *Odyssey* by Livius Andronicus (ca. 284–ca. 204 B.C.), and the *Bellum Punicum* of Cn. Naevius (ca. 270–ca. 201 B.C.). Though Varro (116–27 B.C.) tried to revive the Saturnian in his *Menippean Satires*, it ceased to be a living artistic verse form after Naevius. But it survived in inscriptions. There is fairly general agreement among modern scholars that the Saturnian is an indigenous Italic verse form, in which Latin poetry was cast before the meters of Greek verse were taken over, and that a caesura (see below, section IV) divides the Saturnian line into two slightly uneven parts, of which the first part is longer.

But the question whether the rhythm of the Saturnian was determined by quantities or by natural word accent is far from settled. However, most Saturnians make some kind of sense if we assume that the natural word accent alone carries the rhythm. Thus the first part of a Saturnian line has three naturally accented syllables and the second part two. The number of syllables intervening between the accented syllables is indeterminate. Occasionally a short word may have no accent at all and a long word may have two.

Examples:

málum dábunt Metélli   Naévio poétae
(Keil VI. 266. 16)

vírum míhi, Caména,   ínsece versútum
(Livius Andronicus, *Odissia,* fr. 1 *ROL* II)

tópper cít(i) ad aédis   vénimus Circái   (*Ibid.*, fr. 36)

ímmolábat aúream   víctimam púlchram
(Naevius, *Bellum Punicum,* fr. 4 *ROL* II)

mórs perfécit tu(a) ut éssent   ómnia brévia
(Scipio epitaph in *CIL* I². 2. 10. 2.)

I. Sigla

— longum, i.e., a long element in the scheme = space for one long syllable

∪ breve, i.e., a short element in the scheme = space for one short syllable

× anceps, i.e., space for one long or one short syllable

∧ lack of one element:

  (a) *acephaly* (= "headlessness") at the beginning of Ionic or Aeolic verses (see below, sections XIII and XVI);
  (b) *catalexis*, i.e., suppression of a final element at the end of a period (see below, section III)

61

/ regular recurrence of break, i.e., word ending (see below, section IV)

/ / alternative positions of break

// pause, i.e., end of period (see below, section III)

/// end of strophe (see below, section XVIII)

⌒ bridge, i.e., word ending between two elements avoided or not allowed (see below, section IV)

ia [1]	iamb: ∪ —	} feet used in spoken verse, see below, sections VII and VIII
tro [1]	trochee: — ∪	
ia	iamb: ×— ∪ —	} metra used in lyric verse, see below, section XII
tro	trochee: — ∪ — ×	
cr	cretic: — ∪ —	} see below, section XII
ba	bacchiac: ∪ — —	
lec	lecythion: — ∪ — ∪ — ∪ —	
ith	ithyphallic: — ∪ — ∪ — —	
da	dactyl: — ⏕	
an	anapaest: ⏕ ⏑⏑ ⏕ ⏑⏑	
io	ionic: ∪ ∪ — —	} see below, section XIII
cho	choriamb: — ∪ ∪ —	
anacl	anaclast: ∪ ∪ — ∪ — ∪ — —	
gl	glyconic: × × — ∪ ∪ — ∪ —	} Aeolic meters, see below, section XVI.
ph	pherecratean: × × — ∪ ∪ — —	
hipp	hipponactean: × × — ∪ ∪ — ∪ — —	

II. Metrics and Prosody

Before learning the general rules of Latin prosody, it is essential to realize that the Latin language changed in respect to the syllable quantity within the following epochs: the Early Republic, of which the most important authors were Ennius, Plautus, Terence, and, because of his archaizing tendencies, Lucretius; the Classical Period, which begins roughly with Catullus, and which, though its characteristics

are found in many later writers, may conveniently be re-
garded as ending with the second century A.D.; and finally
Late Latin, both Christian and pagan, from ca. A.D. 200 to
580 (death of Cassiodorus).

1. As in Greek, the quantity (long or short) of a syllable is
determined by the quantity of its vowel. Latin vowels,
accordingly, resemble the Greek vowels in that they are
either long or short, but unlike Greek, Roman writing makes
no distinction between long and short *e* and *o*. Thus the
quantity of the written vowels has to be determined in each
individual case, most conveniently by learning the correct
pronunciation of words at the earliest possible stage or by
consulting a good Latin dictionary.

As in Greek, all diphthongs are long. Closed syllables, i.e.,
syllables which end in a consonant, are treated as metrically
long. Thus ā-mo, but pēr-do. When a closed final syllable
whose vowel is short is followed by a word beginning with a
vowel, the syllable is counted as short, because the final con-
sonant is pronounced with the following word, e.g., flumĕn
altum (because it is pronounced *flume-naltum*). In this con-
nection it should be noted that *x* (= *cs*) and *z* (= *ds*) count
as two consonants, but *qu* as only one, and *h* is not regarded
as a consonant. When a naturally short vowel is followed in
the same word by two consonants the first of which is a mute
(*b, p, d, t, g, c*) and the second a liquid or nasal (*l, m, n, r*) its
syllable may or may not be treated as metrically long. Ovid,
Metamorphoses XIII. 607 (dactylic hexameter, see below,
section V) plays with both:

et primo similis volŭ-cri, mox vera volūc-ris.

However, when the mute closes a syllable, the syllable re-
mains long, e.g. ūt rupes, ōb-lino; but tuă prima, rĕ-trahit, where
the mute belongs to the next syllable.

2. *Hiatus*, i.e., word ending in a vowel or diphthong before word beginning with a vowel or diphthong, is avoided in Latin verse, except that it is occasionally found when a caesura or diaeresis (see below, section IV) separates the two words, e.g., Vergil, *Aeneid* III. 606 (dactylic hexameter, see below, section V):

$$\text{–} \ \cup \ \cup\text{–} \ / \ \cup \ \cup \ \text{–}$$
si pereo, hominum manibus periisse iuvabit.

Note again that initial *h-* is not regarded as a consonant. Hiatus is avoided by means of *elision*, i.e., the final vowel of the first word is only slightly pronounced or altogether suppressed. Final *-m* in Latin was weak (perhaps it was slightly nasalized as in modern French), and the syllable containing it was elided when the following word began with a vowel, e.g., Vergil, *Aeneid* III. 658 (dactylic hexameter, see below, section V):

$$\text{–} \qquad \text{–} \ \text{–} \qquad \text{–} \ \text{–} \qquad \text{–} \ \text{–} \quad \text{–} \ \text{–} \ \cup$$
monstr(um) horrend(um), inform(e), ingens, cui lumen

$$\cup \ \text{–} \qquad \text{–} \ //$$
ademptum.*

When the second word is *es* or *est*, the elision is reversed (= *aphaeresis*) and the *e* of these forms is elided: *dictum (e)st* = *dictumst* (not *dictest*).

Early Latin verse does not avoid hiatus as consistently as does the verse of later periods. Frequently the long final vowel of a monosyllabic word is shortened, but not elided, before a word beginning with a vowel, e.g., Terence, *Hecyra* 343 (iambic septenarius, see below section VII. 2):

$$\qquad\quad \cup \qquad\qquad \cup$$
nam qui amat quoi odi(o) ipsus est, bis facere stulte duco.

* In the Early Republic, final *-s*, and also final *-m*, followed by a word beginning with a consonant, did not necessarily make a syllable closed, e.g., *Oratius inclutu(s) saltu* (Ennius, *Annales* 129 Vahlen [= fr.132 *ROL I*]). While some editors drop the *-s* (or *-m*) in such cases and write *inclutu'*, this practice will not be followed in this book, and we bracket the *-s* instead.

3. *Synizesis*, i.e., the treatment of two adjoining vowels in the same word as one, is found in Latin as it is in Greek: (*deînde, eâdem*). Related to this is the occasional use of *i* and *u* as virtual consonants (pronounced as *y* and *w* respectively): *Lāvīnĭăquĕ vĕnīt* (Vergil, *Aeneid* I. 2), *gĕnŭă lăbānt* (ibid., V. 432). The reverse process also occurs for metrical purposes (a kind of diaeresis): *huïc* has two syllables in, e.g., Statius, *Silvae* I. 1. 107, and *sil-u-ae* three syllables in, e.g., Horace, *Odes* I. 23. 4.

4. A phenomenon that is unknown in Greek but very common in many meters of early Latin poetry is the law of *brevis brevians* or "iambic shortening", found especially in iambs and trochees. According to this law, a long syllable, if preceded by a short syllable, *may* be counted as short if the natural word accent falls on the syllable immediately preceding or following it (i.e., (a) ◡́ — becomes ◡́ ◡, or (b) ◡ — × becomes ◡ ◡ ×́). E.g., (a) in Terence, *Eunuchus* 8 (iambic senarius, see below, section VII. 1):

— — — ◡ ◡ ◡ — — — — — ◡ — //
ex Graecis bonis Latinas fecit non bonas,

the final syllable of *bonis*, though long by nature, is counted as short because the word accent falls on *bo-* preceding it; and (b) in Terence, *Eunuchus* 22 (iambic senarius, see below, section VII. 1):

◡ ◡ — ◡ ◡ ◡ ◡ — ◡ — — — ◡ — //
magistratu(s) quom ib(i) adesset occeptast agi. . . .

the second syllable of *magistratus* is long because it is closed, but it is regarded as short, because the word accent falls on the following *a*.

A special case of (b) occurs when a short monosyllabic word, or a dissyllabic word of which the first syllable is short and the second elided, changes a following long into a short syllable, e.g., Plautus, *Aulularia* 483 (iambic senarius, see below, section VII. 1):

$$\cup\cup - \cup - - \cup\cup - - \cup\cup - \cup - /\!/$$
et illae malam rem metuant quam metuont magis.

In this example, the first syllable of *illae* is short after the short monosyllabic *et*.

III. The Period

Although the periods of Latin poetry are formed in the same way as they arc in Greek (see *Greek Meters*, section 3), it might be useful to recapitulate the most essential features here.

Periods, i.e., what usually appears as lines in printed editions, are separated from one another by means of pauses. These pauses are marked by one or more of the following:

1. *word ending*, which is mandatory. A period never ends in the middle of a word, except that occasionally the final vowel especially of an enclitic, such as the *-e* of *-que* or *-ne*, may be elided if the following period begins with a vowel;

2. *hiatus*. The final vowel in a period is not elided before a period beginning with a vowel, except as stated under 1. above;

3. *brevis in longo*. Although every period ends in a long element, a short syllable may be used at the end of a verse, e.g., Vergil, *Aeneid* I. 16–18 (dactylic hexameter, see below, section V):

$$- /\!/$$
hic illius arma,
$$- /\!/$$
hic currus fuit; hoc regnum dea gentibus esse,
$$- /\!/$$
si qua fata sinant, iam tum tenditque fovetque.

Although the final element in dactylic hexameters is long, each of these lines ends in a short syllable;

4. *catalexis* (= "coming to an abrupt end"). The final element of a meter may be suppressed; a short element preceding it will then be automatically lengthened. For example, the trochaic septenarius (see below, section VIII. 1) is a catalectic meter, consisting of eight trochaic feet with the last element suppressed.

IV. Caesura and Diaeresis

The terms caesura and diaeresis denote the same phenomena in Latin as they do in Greek verse, see above, *Greek Meters*, section 4. However, in view of their importance for a proper understanding of Latin poetry, we shall recapitulate the most essential points here, and at the same time note some of the peculiar features of Latin verse.

In addition to exhibiting a regular sequence of long and short syllables, poetic rhythm in Latin (as well as in Greek) is determined by the fact that at certain places within each given period word ending is either forbidden (or avoided) or required (or recommended). Forbidden word ending is called *bridge*. The place where word ending is demanded is called *caesura* if the break occurs within a metron or foot, and *diaeresis* if the break occurs at the juncture of two metra.

Whereas caesurae and diaereses are not required in the early Greek Aeolic meters, Horace and his successors used them in their imitations of Greek Aeolics, see below, section IX. 2.

V. Spoken Verse: Dactylic Hexameter

Spoken Latin verse is measured in "feet"; Latin lyric verse is measured in "metra". The ancient metricians equated 2 feet with 1 metron. In the case of the dactyl, however, foot and metron were regarded as identical. We shall, therefore, speak of dactylic "feet" when dealing with spoken verse, and of dactylic "metra" in the sections on lyric verse.

The dactylic hexameter (notation: 6 da$_\wedge$//), as in Greek, consists of six dactyls, in which two brevia can always be replaced by one longum. Accordingly, we may speak of trisyllabic ($-\cup\cup$) and dissyllabic ($--$) dactyls. The fifth dactyl is usually trisyllabic and the sixth always dissyllabic.

It was first taken over from the Homeric hexameter by Ennius (239–169 B.C.). The pioneering effort of Ennius has often been regarded with a kind of disdain, a carry-over from the attitude of later Roman poets, especially Horace. As a pioneer he attempted things that were later abandoned, but the attempt had to be made. His failures should not blind the unbiased reader to the beauty of some of his verse nor to the obvious pervasive influence he had on later poets, Lucretius and Vergil in particular. Several devices are immediately evident in Ennius' verse, e.g., the use of alliteration and assonance, which is common to Latin poetry of all periods, e.g., Ennius, *Annales*, 37–38 Vahlen:

> Eurydica prognata, pater quam noster amavit,
> vires vitaque corpu(s) meum nunc deserit omne.

Since Ennius' example did not remain as important for the Latin hexameter as Homer's did for the Greek, changes and improvements were gradually introduced. The *neoterici*, with Catullus' *Peleus and Thetis* (no. 64) as the major example, show some of the developments.* It was left for Vergil to set the definite pattern of the Latin hexameter, and it is from his work that one takes the main examples.

The most common caesura in the Latin hexameter occurs after the third longum, e.g., Vergil, *Aeneid* I. 1:

$$-\ \cup\ \cup\ -\quad \cup\ \cup\ -/\quad --\quad -\quad -\ \cup\ \cup\ --//$$
arma virumque cano, Troiae qui primus ab oris 6 da$_\wedge$//

---

* Lucretius' *De Rerum Natura* is consciously archaic, and is not a true representative of the poetry and poetic movements of the late first century B.C.

The caesura after the fourth longum is also frequent, e.g.,
Vergil, *Georgics* I. 257:

$$- \ - \ - \ - \ - \ \overset{\smile\smile}{} \!-/ \ \smile\smile\!- \ \smile \ \smile - \!-//$$

nec frustra signor(um) obitus speculamur et ortus. 6 da$_\wedge$//

while the caesura after the first breve of the third foot is rare,
e.g., Vergil, *Aeneid* IV. 486:

$$- \ - \ - \ \smile\smile \ -\smile/\smile-\smile\smile - \ \smile \ \smile -\!-//$$

spargens umida mella soporiferumque papaver. 6 da$_\wedge$//

In addition to one of these caesurae, there occurs in some
dactylic hexameters a strong rhetorical break after the fourth
foot, in which the sense joins the last two feet with the follow-
ing verse. This break is called "bucolic diaeresis", because it
is fairly common in Greek (though less in Latin) pastoral
poetry, e.g., Vergil, *Eclogues* VI. 25–26:

$$- \ \smile\smile \ - \ -\!-/ - \ - \smile\smile / - \ \smile\smile \ -\!-//$$

carmina quae vultis cognoscite; carmina vobis,

$$- \ \smile\smile\!- \ -\!-\smile \ \smile\!-$$

huic aliud mercedis erit. . . .

Where this break occurs, the fourth foot is almost always tri-
syllabic. Note also that the bucolic diaeresis is not confined
to pastoral poetry.

In the Vergilian hexameter, a closed syllable before the
caesura may remain long, even though the next word begins
with a vowel, e.g., Vergil, *Aeneid* I. 651:

$$-/$$

Pergama cum peteret inconcessosqu(e) hymenaeos.

Hiatus may shorten a final vowel or diphthong, especially
before words derived from Greek, e.g., Vergil, *Aeneid* III.
211:

$$- \ \smile\smile$$

insulae Ioni(o) in magno, quas dira Celaeno.

Again, unlike the earlier poets, Vergil avoided a mono-
syllable following a caesura after the third longum. This
practice also affected the structure of Horace's imitations of

Greek Aeolic poetry (see below, section XVI). The Latin hexameter, unlike the Greek, avoids a line consisting entirely of dissyllabic feet as well as polysyllabic final words. Normally the line ends in a word of two or three syllables (except for *est*). Monosyllables and two dissyllabic words are avoided at the end of the period, in order not to make the end choppy. The scheme, then, of the last two feet is:

$$\ldots \overset{5}{-} \smallfrown / \cup / \overset{6}{-} \smallfrown \,\underline{}$$

It is curious to note that in this kind of verse ending the natural word accents usually fall on the long elements. In other words, in the last two feet of the dactylic hexameter, word accent and verse rhythm usually coincide. It was probably an awareness of this fact that caused the Roman poets to treat the last two feet of the dactylic hexameter as detachable enough to form a new metrical unit, the so-called *adonic*, and to recognize it in the ending of the Sapphic strophe (see below, section XVIII). Yet it remains debatable whether the prevalence of this kind of verse is to be explained as due to the natural word accent. The fact that hexameter endings such as $\acute{-}/\cup \cup \acute{-}-//$ (e.g. *tum cupientes*) are almost entirely avoided in Latin verse suggests that word accent was not the primary formative element. It seems, rather, that this particular grouping of words, i.e., an accented monosyllable at the fifth longum followed by a tetrasyllabic word accented on the penultimate, sounded offensive to Roman ears at the end of the dactylic hexameter.

Final monosyllables are sometimes employed for specific effects, e.g., Vergil, *Aeneid* I. 105:

dat latus, insequitur cumulo praeruptus aquae mons.

The hexameter of Horace's *Satires* follows the same pattern as that of Vergil, though their relaxed conversational tone makes for some variations. It was Ovid who went even further and gave the hexameter the polished excellence (and some of the monotony) that it kept in Latin from his time on. One interesting development in Ovid is a playful use of rhyme at the caesura and at the end of the line, e.g., Ovid, *Ars Amatoria* I. 59:

> quot caelum stellas, tot habet tua Roma puellas.

Such rhymes are even more common in the second line of the elegiac couplet, which will be discussed in the next section, though there is no evidence that rhyme was sought for itself by the Latin poets. But of course the inflectional endings made it relatively easy to obtain an assonance.

VI. *Spoken Verse: The Elegiac Couplet*

The rules for the first line are the same as those for the dactylic hexameter discussed in section V. The scheme of the second line is the same as that of the Greek (see *Greek Meters*, section 6), a duplication of the hemiepes (= the hexameter taken to its most common caesura after the third longum; notation: 3 da$_{\wedge\wedge}$/) with diaeresis between the two:

$$- \overline{\cup\cup} - \overline{\cup\cup} -/- \cup\cup - \cup\cup -//$$

Note the absence of dissyllabic dactyls (= spondees) in the second half. The "rules" for writing elegiac couplets became more fixed as time went on, and were finally settled with the classic forms of Ovid, where elision is infrequent in the hexameter, and where a monosyllabic or trisyllabic word rarely ends the second line, e.g., Ovid, *Amores* I. 9. 1–2:

$$-\cup\cup \quad - \quad \cup \cup \quad - \ / \ \cup \quad \cup \ - \quad \cup\cup \quad - \quad \cup \quad \cup - -//$$
Militat omnis amans, et habet sua castra Cupido;

$$6 \text{ da}_{\wedge}//$$

$$-\cup\cup \quad - \cup \quad \cup -/ \ -\cup\cup \quad - \quad \cup \cup \quad - \ ///$$
Attice, crede mihi, militat omnis amans.

$$3 \text{ da}_{\wedge\wedge}/3 \text{ da}_{\wedge\wedge}///$$

This example neatly shows the origin of the second line from the hemiepes (3 da$_{\wedge\wedge}$/).

The elegiac couplet after Catullus is invariably a grammatical unit, and there is no carry-over to the next couplet. Within the couplet, there are often grammatical connections between the "halves", both of the hexameter and the second line, e.g., Tibullus I. 1. 1–2:

$$- \cup \cup - \cup \cup - \ \ - - / \cup \cup \ - \ \ \cup \cup \ - - \ //$$
Divitias alius *fulvo* sibi congerat *auro*
$$- \ \cup \cup - - - / - \cup \cup \ \ - \cup \ \cup - \ ///$$
et teneat *culti* iugera multa *soli.*

In both lines the adjective stands before the caesura or diaeresis and the noun at the end of the line.

VII. Spoken Verse: Iambic Meters

The major representatives of early dramatic verse are the comedies of Plautus and Terence. Of the other dramatic poets, both comic and tragic, contemporary with the two mentioned, we possess only fragments.

Latin dramatic verse is further removed from its Greek prototypes than is epic verse. While Greek verse is measured in metra, Latin spoken poetry, as we saw in section V above, counts the foot as the basic unit. Thus the Latin equivalent of the Greek iambic trimeter (3 metra) is the iambic senarius (6 feet); the tetrameter (4 metra) corresponds to the octonarius (8 feet).

Latin comedy distinguishes the types of meter employed into *diverbia* and *cantica*, "dialogues" and "songs", depending on whether the words are accompanied by instrumental music or not. *Cantica* are further subdivided into recitative passages (*cantica*) and those actually sung (*mutatis modis cantica*). We shall leave the *mutatis modis cantica*, usually referred to simply as *cantica*, for later consideration (see below, sections IX and XIX) and confine our attention in this section and the next to spoken and recitative verse.

The comic meters, then, were a free adaptation of the Greek models. If we compare the earliest extant Latin verse written under Greek influence, the iambs and trochees of Plautus and Terence, with their Greek models, we find that the Romans were apparently not as sensitive to the difference between anceps and breve as were the Greeks. In the early Latin iambs and trochees, brevia are so much treated like ancipitia that either a long or two short syllables may be used where in Greek a breve is mandatory. The net result is that a Latin iambic or trochaic verse *may* consist entirely of short or – except for the next-to-last (or third last) syllable, which must be short – entirely of long syllables. How did the contemporaries of Plautus and Terence hear the iambic or trochaic rhythm of such verses? To some extent, they would of course be helped by the metrical context in which such a verse would be found: if a line consisting, let us say, of 22 short syllables is found in a speech consisting entirely of iambic senarii, the presumption is that that verse is to be taken as an iambic senarius, resolved into short syllables for the sake of variation. Moreover, the fact that Latin permits so much freedom in resolution as compared with Greek is probably due to differences in the structure of the two languages. This, however, still does not answer the question *how* the Romans of the second century B.C. heard the iambic or trochaic rhythm in verses in which the sequence of long and short syllables alone would not automatically indicate an iambic or trochaic rhythm. Although certainty cannot be attained, many modern scholars believe that regard for the natural word accent helped carry the rhythm of early Latin verse – and perhaps also of later Latin poetry – sufficiently to make the basic pattern intelligible even where the sequence

73

of long and short syllables did not. This view is supported by the fact that iambic shortening (see above, section II. 4) is extremely common in comic iambs and trochees. The precise extent of this regard for the natural word accent is, however, hard to define.

1. *Iambic senarius* (notation: ia⁶ //) . The very name of this meter, which is based on the Greek 3 ia// (see *Greek Meters*, section 7), indicates that in iambic verse the Romans counted feet and not metra. The basic form of the meter as employed by Plautus is:

$$\overset{\cup\cup}{\underset{\cup}{}} \overset{}{\underset{}{\cup\cup}}, \overset{\cup\cup}{\underset{\cup}{}} \overset{}{\underset{}{\cup\cup}}, \overset{\cup\cup}{\underset{\cup}{}}/\overset{}{\underset{}{\cup\cup}}, \overset{\cup\cup}{\underset{\cup}{}}/\overset{}{\underset{}{\cup\cup}}, \overset{\cup\cup}{\underset{\cup}{}} \overset{}{\underset{}{\cup\cup}}, \quad \cup - \; //$$

Note that the caesura follows the model of the Greek trimeter, occurring in the third or fourth foot.

We see here that the iambic senarius is much freer than its Greek equivalent. Its iambic character seems to be determined only by the fact that Plautus was careful to distinguish the last from the other feet. The fifth is a pure iamb *only* if it starts a word or phrase which leads into the sixth. E.g., Plautus, *Asinaria* 19:

```
  —      — —    — — / ∪ ∪∪ — — — — ∪ — //
perqu(e) illam quam tu metuis uxorem tuam.      ia⁶ //
```

or Plautus, *Casina* 771:

```
 —  ∪ ∪ —  ∪ ∪ —/ — ∪ ∪  —    ∪ ∪ —  ∪ —//
sed nimium lepide dissimulant, quasi nil sciant,   ia⁶ //
```

but with iambic fifth foot, Plautus, *Aulularia* 576:

```
 —    —    ∪  ∪ ∪    — / —  — — ∪ — ∪ — //
post hoc quod habe(o) ut commutet coloniam.     ia⁶ //
```

The senarius as employed by Phaedrus differs from that of Plautus and Terence only in the fact that Phaedrus did not make use of the principle of iambic shortening, see above, section II. 4.

It is obvious that the many forms which the iambic senarius (and the other spoken dramatic meters) can assume make it very difficult for the student to read them with the ease, say, of the hexameter or elegiac distich. There are several practical ways of overcoming this difficulty. One (a) is to regard the Latin iamb like the English and thus stress every even syllable (or in case of a resolved even syllable, the first of the two shorts), e.g.,

> sed nímium lépide díssimulánt, quasi níl sciánt.

This clearly gives the six "beats" to the line. Another possibility (b) is to set the stress to follow the natural word accent, e.g.,

> séd nímium lépide dissímulant, quási níl scíant,

allowing the accentual pattern to establish the type of verse. These same methods can be followed with the other types of Latin spoken verse, and might be especially successful with the trochaic septenarius (see below, section VIII. 1), which has an English equivalent (cf. Tennyson, *Locksley Hall*).

Whatever the merits of accent by metrical "beat" (a) may have, such as creating in the English ear the effect of a six-foot iambic line, it necessarily misrepresents the regular pronunciation of classical Latin. The latter method (b) will follow the rules of Latin word accent, but the extent to which word accent played a role in this kind of Latin verse remains doubtful. It must be admitted, nevertheless, that Latin accent in the time of Plautus and Terence was only moving in the direction of the fixed Penultimate Law. The early poets made some compromises between the new tendencies of the language, its former free accent, and the exigencies of the adapted Greek structures. There are confusions for the modern scholar in dealing with early Latin meters, and no

75

theory has yet been put forward which explains all the divergencies between these early Latin meters and their corresponding Greek models.

2. *Iambic septenarius* (notation: ia ^{7} //). This verse is usually divided in two by a diaeresis after the fourth foot. This diaeresis is so strong in Plautus that the line is felt to be two separate entities. Thus hiatus and *brevis in longo* are allowed at this point. The fourth and seventh feet are usually iambic. In Terence, hiatus and *brevis in longo* are less frequent at the diaeresis, and a caesura within the fifth foot often replaces the diaeresis.

Scheme:

$$\underset{\smile}{\smile\smile} \underset{}{\smile\smile}\underline{}, \underset{\smile}{\smile\smile} \underset{}{\smile\smile}\underline{}, \underset{\smile}{\smile\smile} \underset{}{\smile\smile}\underline{}, \smile\underline{}, / \underset{\smile}{\overset{\smile\smile}{}} / \smile\smile, \underset{}{\smile\smile}\underline{}, \underset{\smile}{\smile\smile\smile\smile}, \underline{} //$$

Examples: Terence, *Phormio* 756:

$$\underline{} \ \smile\smile\underline{} \ \underline{} \ \underline{} \ \underline{} \ \smile \ \underline{} \ / \ \smile \ \underline{} \ \smile \ \underline{}\smile \ \underline{} \ \underline{}//$$

composito factumst quo mod(o) hanc amans habere posset

ia ^{7} //

hiatus: Plautus, *Asinaria* 381:

$$\underline{} \ \underline{} \ \underline{} \ \underline{}\underline{} \ \underline{} \ \smile\underline{}/ \ \underline{} \ \underline{} \ \underline{} \ \underline{} \ \smile \ \underline{} \ \underline{}//$$

ut demonstratae sunt mihi, hasc(e) aedis ess(e) oportet

ia ^{7} //

caesura in fifth foot: Terence, *Eunuchus* 288:

$$\smile\underline{}\underline{} \ \underline{} \ \underline{} \ \underline{}\smile \ \underline{} \ \underline{}/\underline{}\smile\underline{} \ \underline{} \ \smile \ \smile\underline{}//$$

facete dictum: mira vero militi qui placeat?   ia ^{7} //

3. *Iambic octonarius* (notation: ia ^{8} //). This meter is identical with the iambic septenarius, except that it has one element more. If there is no diaeresis after the fourth foot, there is normally a caesura in the fifth:

$$\underset{\smile}{\smile\smile} \underset{}{\smile\smile}\underline{}, \underset{\smile}{\smile\smile} \underset{}{\smile\smile}\underline{}, \underset{\smile}{\smile\smile} \underset{}{\smile\smile}\underline{}, \smile\underline{}, / \underset{\smile}{\overset{\smile\smile}{}} / \smile\smile, \underset{}{\smile\smile}\underline{}, \underset{\smile}{\smile\smile\smile\smile}, \smile\underline{} //$$

Example: Plautus, *Amphitruo* 1053:

$$\underline{} \ \underline{} \ \smile \ \underline{} \ \underline{} \ \underline{} \ \smile\underline{}/\smile \ \underline{} \ \smile \ \underline{} \ \underline{} \ \underline{} \ \smile\underline{}//$$

spes atqu(e) opes vitae meae iacent sepult(ae) in pectore. . . .

ia ^{8} //

76

One finds the other type in Plautus, though Terence is more fond of it, e.g., Terence, *Andria* 199:

$$\text{—} \cup \cup \cup \quad \text{—} \text{—} \quad \text{—} \text{—} \text{—} \text{—}/ \text{—} \cup \text{—}$$
$$\overline{\text{verberibu(s) caesum t(e) in pistrinum, Dave, ded(am)}}$$

$$\text{—} \quad \text{—} \cup \text{—} //$$
$$\overline{\text{usqu(e) ad necem.}} \quad \text{ia}\,8\,//$$

VIII. Spoken Verse: Trochaic Meters

1. The *trochaic septenarius* (notation: tro⁷ //)   is the only trochaic meter used in dialogue proper. It is Plautus' favorite meter. The scheme shows that it is actually a cata-lectic eight-foot meter despite the name:

$$\underline{\cup\cup} \ \overset{\cup\cup}{\underline{\cup}}, \ \underline{\cup\cup} \ \overset{\cup\cup}{\underline{\cup}}, \ \underline{\cup\cup} \ \overset{\cup\cup}{\underline{\cup}}, \ \underline{\cup\cup}/\overset{(\cup\cup)}{}, \ /\underline{\cup\cup} \ \overset{\cup\cup}{\underline{\cup}}, \ \underline{\cup\cup} \ \overset{\cup\cup}{\underline{\cup}}, \ \underline{\cup\cup} \ \cup, \ \text{—}//$$

Most common is the diaeresis after the fourth foot, but caesura within the fourth foot is also found. E.g., Plautus, *Poenulus* 864:

$$\text{—} \quad \text{—} \quad \text{—} \quad \text{—} \quad \text{—} \quad \text{—} \quad \text{—} \quad \text{—} \quad \text{—}/ \cup\cup\cup \quad \text{—} \quad \text{—}$$
$$\text{me non perdent; ill(um) ut perdant facere possum,}$$

$$\text{—} \cup \text{—} //$$
$$\text{si velim,} \qquad \text{tro}\,7\,//$$

or Plautus, *Amphitruo* 286:

$$\text{—} \cup\cup \text{—} \quad \cup\cup \text{—} \cup \quad \text{—} / \text{—} \cup \cup \text{—} \text{—} \text{—} \text{—} \cup \text{—}//$$
$$\text{accipiam; modo sis ven(i) huc: invenies infortunium.}$$

$$\text{tro}\,7\,//$$

The trochaic septenarius is not only common in Plautus and Terence, but throughout the history of Roman poetry it remained one of the most popular meters. Seneca used it in three passages (*Medea* 740–751, *Oedipus* 223–232, and *Phaedra* 1201–1212). Outside drama, it appears, for example, in Ennius' *Epicharmus*, fr. 56 Vahlen:

$$\text{—} \quad \text{—} \quad \text{—} \cup \quad \text{—} \cup \quad \text{—}/ \text{—} \cup \quad \text{—} \text{—} \quad \text{—} \cup \text{—} //$$
$$\overline{\text{atqu(e) ex imbre frigu(s) ventu(s)}} \text{ post fit aer denuo}$$

$$\text{tro}\,7\,//$$

Its non-literary or popular uses are quite common in riddles, popular satiric pieces, and soldiers' songs, where it is also

called the *versus quadratus*, e.g., a soldiers' song at the Gallic
triumph of Julius Caesar in Suetonius, *Divus Iulius* 51:

— ⏑⏑ — ⏑⏑   — ⏑⏑ — / — — — —   — — ⏑ —//
urbani, servat(e) uxores, moechum calv(um) adducimus.

tro⁷//

—   — — ⏑   — ⏑⏑ — —/ — —   — — — ⏑ —//
aui(um) in Galli(a) effutuisti, hic sumpsisti mutuum.

tro ⁷//

It occurs again in that most beautiful of later Latin poems,
the *Pervigilium Veneris* 89–90, 93:

— ⏑ — —   — ⏑ — —/ — ⏑ —   ⏑ —   ⏑ —//
illa cantat. nos tacemus. quando ver venit meum?

tro⁷//

— ⏑ —   ⏑ —   ⏑ — —/ — ⏑ — ⏑ — ⏑ — //
quando fi(am) uti chelidon ut tacere desinam? . . .

tro⁷ //

— ⏑ —   — —   ⏑ — —/ —   ⏑ — —
cras amet qui numqu(am) amavit quiqu(e) amavit

— ⏑ —//
cras amet.   tro⁷//

It is the meter of some of the finest Latin hymns, beginning
with St Hilary of Poitiers (d. A.D. 367), *Hymn* 3. 4:

— — — — — ⏑ —   —/ — —   — ⏑ — ⏑ —//
hostis fallax saeculor(um) et dirae mortis artifex.

Another example is Venantius Fortunatus' hymn "Pange
lingua" 22–24:

— ⏑ — ⏑   — ⏑ —   —/— ⏑ — ⏑ —⏑—//
crux fidelis, inter omnes arbor una nobilis —

— ⏑ — —   — ⏑   — —/ — ⏑ —   ⏑ — ⏑—//
nulla talem silva profert flore fronde germine —

— ⏑ — —   — ⏑   — —/— ⏑   — —   — ⏑—//
dulce lignum dulce clavo dulce pondus sustinens.

2. The *trochaic octonarius* (notation: tro⁸//) appears rarely
in the comic poets (about 150 lines in Plautus and about 90 in
Terence), and is employed in recitative scenes of great ex-

citement. Like its iambic equivalent, it has a diaeresis after the fourth foot:

$$\cup\cup\ \overset{\cup\cup}{\underset{\cup}{-}},\ \cup\cup\ \overset{\cup\cup}{\underset{\cup}{-}},\ \cup\cup\ \overset{\cup\cup}{\underset{\cup}{-}},\ \cup\cup\ \underset{\cup}{-},\ /\cup\cup\ \overset{\cup\cup}{\underset{\cup}{-}},\ \cup\cup\ \overset{\cup\cup}{\underset{\cup}{-}},\ \cup\cup\ \overset{\cup\cup}{\underset{\cup}{-}},\ \cup\cup\ -//$$

E.g., Plautus, *Aulularia* 406–407:

$$- \cup -\quad -- \quad \cup\ \cup -- / - \cup \quad\quad - \cup$$
attatae! cives, populares, incol(ae), accol(ae),

$$- \quad \cup \quad\quad - \quad\quad - \ //$$
adven(ae) omnes,   tro[8] //

$$\cup\cup\ \cup- \quad\quad - \cup\ \cup\cup\ \cup\cup-/\ \cup\cup\cup\ -- \quad \cup\cup- \quad \cup\cup-//$$
date viam qua fugere liceat, facite totae plateae pateant.

tro[8] //

IX. Lyric Poetry

In the preceding sections (V–VIII), we have discussed those Latin meters which are derived from Greek spoken verse. We now turn to those derived from Greek sung verse, which we shall call "lyric" poetry. The meters with which we shall be concerned here are composed in the Greek way by metra rather than by feet, as the spoken meters are. In this area, Greek poetry exercised two kinds of influence upon the Romans: 1. The lyric parts of Greek drama were utilized by Plautus in the composition of his *cantica*. In this connection, it is interesting to observe that Terence used lyric meters to any significant extent only in his *Adelphoe* and *Andria*. 2. Catullus and Horace drew exclusively upon the meters used by the Greek lyric poets, and Seneca followed the practices of Horace in composing the lyric parts of his tragedies.

1. Music and song were much more part of the Roman theater than they were of the Greek. In their adaptations from the Greek, Roman dramatists sometimes changed spoken parts of the Greek original into arias. Moreover, in addition to many songs, Roman comedies are filled with recitatives which, though written in iambic septenarii or

79

octonarii (see section VII) and in trochaic septenarii (see section VIII), meters closely related to spoken verse, were not spoken but declaimed to the accompaniment of a flute. Incidentally, we know the names of two Roman dramatic composers, whose work, however, is lost: Marcippor Oppi wrote the music for Plautus' *Stichus*, and Flaccus Claudi composed music for some of Terence's comedies.

While most Greek dramatic lyric poetry is choral, the *cantica* of Roman drama, except for Seneca's tragedies, consist exclusively of solos, which can be sung consecutively by two, three, four, or even five actors. Similarly, the strophic structure with its responsion (see *Greek Meters*, section 18), which is the backbone of the lyric parts of Greek drama, is practically unknown among the Romans. Seneca, however, wrote his *cantica* primarily for choruses (but also as solos), and modelled his meters upon those of Horace's lyrics. If any music accompanied his dramas, it was presumably that of his own time and not identical with the music composed for the comedies of Plautus and Terence.

2. The most striking difference between the lyrics of Catullus and Horace and those of their Greek predecessors is that, with a few exceptions, Latin lyric poems seem to have been spoken rather than sung; lyrics set to music seem to have been rare. We have positive information only about the fact that Horace's *Carmen Saeculare* was sung; but it is quite likely that some of the hymns of Catullus (e.g., no. 34) and Horace (e.g., *Odes* I. 21) were originally written to be sung.

One of the most striking consequences of the use of Greek sung periods for Latin spoken verse is the appearance of regular caesurae in Latin Aeolic meters (see below, section XVI) from Horace on. At the same time, there develops a tendency in Latin Aeolics to allow only longa where the corresponding periods in early Greek poetry have ancipitia.

Like Greek non-dramatic lyric, its Latin counterpart generally consists of strophes, each of which is composed of several periods and metra which may or may not be limited to one form of meter. Moreover, there is a tendency in Latin lyrics to regularize the length of strophes and to use some lines in stichic sequence, i.e., to repeat the same period without any change, as in spoken iambic senarii, dactylic hexameters, etc.; see above, sections V–VIII. By the same token, in Horace's *Odes* the number of lines in each ode can be considered as divisible by 4 (= Meineke's Law, see below, section XVIII), the only exception being *Odes* IV. 8. Asclepiadeans, ionics, iambic trimeters, and dactylic tetrameters may serve for stichic compositions. See also below, section XVIII.

X. Lyric Dactyls

The lyric dactyls in Latin resemble those in Greek in that double brevia are replaced by longa less frequently than they are in the hexameters of epic and satire. However, Latin lyric dactyls display considerably less variety in form than do the Greek. They occur only in hexameters, tetrameters, and as hemiepes.

Hexameters are found in combination with dactylic tetrameters, the hemiepes, and iambs. They are especially common in Horace's *Epodes*. For the structure of this verse, see above, section V.

Tetrameters are used with the last metron either dissyllabic or trisyllabic. Tetrameters with dissyllabic ending (notation: 4 da⁻//) occur in Horace only in combination with dactylic hexameters. After Horace, Ausonius, Prudentius, and Boethius used them also for stichic compositions. The two brevia may be replaced by a long syllable in any metron but the third (exception: Horace, *Odes* I. 28. 2:

81

ᵘᵘ⁻ ⁻ ⁻⁻
cohibent, Archyta). There is no regular caesura or diaeresis.
E.g., Horace, *Odes* I. 7. 1–2:

laudabunt alii claram Rhodon aut Mytilenen   6 da$_\wedge$//
aut Epheson bimarisve Corinthi. . . .   4 da⁻//

Cf. also Horace, *Odes* I. 28 and *Epodes* 12.

Tetrameters with trisyllabic last metron (notation: 4 da᷂/)
permit the substitution of a long syllable for two brevia
in the first three metra. This type of dactylic tetrameter,
with trisyllabic final metron, appears to echo the rhythm
of the dactylic hexameter taken to the bucolic diaeresis
(see above, section V). It is used in combination with
hexameters by Boethius, *De Consolatione Philosophiae* I. 3;
but otherwise primarily in stichic sequence, e.g., in Seneca's
Oedipus 449–465; *Hercules Oetaeus* 1947–1962. One of the
earliest uses of stichic tetrameters is in Ennius' *Alexander*,
fr. VI, lines 50–53 *SRF*:

iamque mari magno classis cita   4 da᷂/
texitur: exiti(um) examen rapit;   4 da᷂/
adveniet fera velivolantibu(s)   4 da᷂/
navibu(s) complebit manu(s) litora.   4 da᷂/

The hemiepes (3 da$_\wedge$/) has been explained in section VI,
above. Elision is not permitted and dissyllabic dactyls are
rare. Horace uses it in combination with the dactylic hexa-
meter in *Odes* IV. 7, see below, section XV. 1. Cf. also
Ausonius IV. 26 and IX. 2. Ausonius also uses the hemiepes
by itself in stichic sequence in V. 10.

XI. Anapaests

As in Greek, longum and double breve are equivalent and
can be substituted anywhere for one another. However, in

the anapaests of Seneca's tragedies only the first longum of a metron can be replaced by two brevia. While in the dimeters of Seneca and his successors (Ausonius, Claudian, and Boethius) diaeresis regularly separates the two metra, diaeresis is common, but not required, in the dimeters of old tragedy and in Palutus. Iambic shortening (see above, section II. 4) is very common in the anapaests of Plautus. There are no anapaests in the surviving plays of Terence.

Seneca is fond of concluding a series of anapaestic dimeters with an anapaestic monometer as a clausula; old tragedy and comedy, on the other hand, follow the Greek pattern more closely in that they prefer a catalectic dimeter (= paroemiac; notation: 2 an∧//) as a clausula. E.g., Plautus, *Aulularia* 721–726:

— — ∪∪ — / ∪∪— ∪∪–//	
heu me miserum, misere perii,	2 an//
∪∪ — ∪∪ — ∪ ∪ —∪ ∪—//	
male perditu(s), pessum(e) ornatus eo:	2 an//
— — ∪ ∪ —/ ∪∪ — ∪∪—/	
tantum gemit(i) et mali maestitiaequ(e)	2 an/
— ⌢ — ∪∪ / ∪ ∪ — ∪∪—//	
hic dies m(i) optulit, fam(em) et pauperiem.	2 an//
∪∪— ∪ ∪ ∪ ∪/ — — — —//	
peritissumus ego s(um) omni(um) in terra;	2 an//
— — ∪ ∪ — — — —//	
nam quid m(i) opust vita, tant(um) auri	2 an//
— ∪∪ — — — — —//	
perdidi, quod concustodivi	2 an//
— ∪ ∪ — — — — — — //	
sedul(o) egomet me defrudav(i)	2 an//
∪ ∪ — ∪ ∪—/ ∪∪ — ∪ ∪ — //	
animumque meum geniumque meum;	2 an//
— ∪∪∪∪–/—∪∪— — //	
nunc eo alii laetificantur	2 an//
∪∪ ∪ ∪ — — ∪∪ ∪ ∪—///	
meo mal(o) et damno. pati nequeo.	2 an∧///

The paroemiac is also found in stichic compositions of Ausonius, Prudentius, and Boethius. Anapaestic tetrameters, consisting of two consecutive dimeters combined in one period, are not uncommon in Plautus, usually in catalectic form, e.g., Plautus, *Persa* 777:

$$\text{— —} \quad \cup\cup\text{—} \quad \text{— } \cup \cup\text{——} \quad \text{— } \cup$$
qui sunt, qui erunt quique fuerunt quique
$$\cup\text{———} \quad \text{— —}//$$
futuri sunt posthac, . . . 4 an$_\wedge$//

XII. *Lyric Iambs, Trochees, Cretics, and Bacchiacs*

Lyrics iambs and trochees are very common in Roman comedy; but they are not mixed with cretics and bacchiacs as frequently as they are in Greek drama. However, iambic and trochaic periods usually alternate with iambic and trochaic periods of different length: e.g. in Horace, *Epodes* 2, an iambic trimeter alternates with an iambic dimeter. Moreover, while sequences composed entirely in cretics and bacchiacs are rare in early Greek, they are very common in Plautus. Latin lyric iambs and trochees differ from those of spoken verse in that they follow the Greek pattern more closely and are composed in metra rather than in feet, except for comedy, where the habit of composing spoken verse in feet also carried over into sung verse.

1. *Iambs.* The trimeter resembles the Greek scheme: $\times\text{—}\cup\text{—}, \times \text{!—}\cup\text{!—}, \times\text{—}\cup\text{—}//$; two short syllables may take the place of any longum, except of course the last. As in Greek, a caesura occurs after the second anceps or the second breve. Verses without caesura are very rare. Here belongs also the so-called "pure iambic trimeter", in which all ancipitia are short and no resolutions of the longa permitted.

Examples: (a) trimeter with resolutions, Horace, *Epodes* 17. 65:

$$\text{— —} \quad \cup\text{——}/ \quad \cup\cup\cup \quad \text{———} \quad \cup\text{—}//$$
uptat quietem Pelopis infidi pater   3 ia//

(b) pure trimeter, Catullus, no. 4. 1:

$$\cup-\cup\ -\cup/\ \ -\ \ \cup-\cup\ -\ \cup-//$$
phaselus ille, quem videtis, hospites,　　3 ia//

An iambic trimeter with a longum in place of the last breve, i.e. with ending $\cup---//$ instead of $\cup-\cup-//$ as in the normal trimeter, is called a *choliamb* (= "lame iamb") or *scazon* (= "limping verse"). It was first used by the Greek poet Hipponax (sixth century B.C.). Choliambs (= chol//) in stichic sequence are one of the favorite meters of Catullus, e.g., no. 8. 1:

$$\cup-\ \ \cup-\cup/\ -\cup-\ \cup--\ --//$$
miser Catulle, desinas ineptire.　　chol//

They are also found in Vergil's *Catalepton*, in Petronius, and Martial.

Further, we find catalectic iambic trimeters (notation: 3 ia$_\wedge$//) in combination with different verses in two poems of Horace (*Odes* I. 4 and II. 18).

Horace uses iambic dimeters only in the *Epodes*, where they are combined with other verse forms; in comedy (where their structure is rather that of four iambic feet, cf. above, section VII) and in Seneca's tragedies they are also used in stichic sequence. E.g., Plautus, *Epidicus* 27–28:

$$\cup\ -\ \ \ \ -\ --\ \cup-//$$
at un(um) a praetura tua,　　　　ia^4//

$$\cup\ \cup\cup\ \ \cup\ -\ \ \ \ -\ \ \ \cup-//$$
Epidic(e), abest. – quidnam? – scies:　ia^4//

$$---\ \ \cup\cup\ \cup\ \ -\ \cup-//$$
lictores duo, du(o) ulmei　　　　ia^4//

$$-\ -\ --\ \ \ \ -\ \cup-//$$
fasces virgarum. – vae tibi!　　　ia^4//

In Horace and his successors the brevia remain short, e.g., Horace, *Epodes* 1. 2:

$$\cup\ -\cup\ \ --\ -\cup-//$$
amice, propugnacula　　　　2 ia//

or *Epodes* 2. 14:

$$-- \cup --- \cup -//$$
feliciores inserit 2 ia//

or Seneca, *Agamemno* 759–762:

$$- - \cup -- - \cup -//$$
instant sorores squalidae 2 ia//

$$- \cup\cup\cup -- - \cup -//$$
sanguinea iactant verbera, 2 ia//

$$- - \cup --- \cup -//$$
fert laeva scmustas faces 2 ia//

$$- - \cup --- \cup -//$$
turgentque pallentes genae. . . . 2 ia//

Catullus once uses a catalectic iambic tetrameter, consisting of three iambs + bacchiac, with regular diaeresis after the second metron: Catullus, no. 25. 12–13:

$$\cup - \cup - \cup - \cup -/ \cup - \cup - \cup - - //$$
et insolenter aestues, velut minuta magno 4 ia$_\wedge$//

$$- - \cup - \cup - \cup -/ --\cup - \cup - - //$$
deprensa navis in mari, vesaniente vento. 4 ia$_\wedge$//

2. *Trochees* show less variety than iambs. What is frequently called catalectic trochaic tetrameter is sometimes better interpreted as a trochaic septenarius, see above, section VIII. 1.

Acatalectic trochaic dimeters are to be construed as the second half of trochaic octonarii (see above, section VIII. 2), but do not as frequently permit the resolution of one into two brevia. E.g., Plautus, *Persa* 29a–31:

$$- - \cup \cup - \cup\cup - - -//$$
quid iam? – qui(a) erus peregri (e)st. – ain tu, tro⁴ //

$$\cup \cup - - - \cup\cup \cup -- //$$
peregri (e)st? – si tut' tibi ben(e) esse tro⁴ //

$$\cup\cup \cup - \cup\cup -- -- //$$
pote pati, veni: vives mecum, tro⁴ //

$$\cup\cup\cup - \cup \cup - \cup --//$$
basilic(o) accipiere victu. tro⁴ //

3. *Bacchiacs and Cretics.* Stichic compositions of bacchiac or cretic* tetrameters or dimeters, both in acatalectic and catalectic form, are frequent in Roman drama. Iambic shortening and synizesis (see above, section II. 3 and 4) are very rare.

In bacchiacs, unlike the Greek, one long or two short syllables may take the place of the breve, and either of the longa may be resolved into two short syllables. Catalectic and acatalectic bacchiac tetrameters are often used in the same scheme, here with iambic clausula: Plautus, *Mostellaria* 84–90:

recordatu(s) mult(um) et diu cogitavi   4 ba//

argumentaqu(e) in pectus mult(a) institui   4 ba//

eg(o), atqu(e) in meo corde, si (e)st quod mihi cor, 4 ba//

eam rem volutav(i) et diu disputavi,   4 ba//

hominem quoiiu(s) rei, quando natus est   4 baʌ//

simil(em) ess(e) arbitrarer simulacrumqu(e) habere 4 ba//

  id repperi i(am) exemplum.   2 iaʌ///

Acatalectic bacchiac dimeters are also frequently found as clausulae of bacchiac systems, e.g., Plautus, *Trinummus* 232:

        ad aetat(em) agundam.   2 ba//

Cretics occur most commonly in acatalectic tetrameters, usually with diaeresis after the second metron, e.g., Plautus, *Rudens* 271:

    fan(um) ad istunc modum non veniri solet.   4 cr//

---

* As in Greek, cretics can always be mixed with their resolved forms, first paeons (—∪∪∪) or fourth paeons (∪∪∪—).

While catalectic cretic tetrameters are rare, a curtailed form of the cretic tetrameter which ends in $-\widebar{\cup}-\cup-//$ is found frequently, e.g., Plautus, *Bacchides* 663–664:

$$\overline{-}\;\overset{\cup}{}\;\overline{-}\;\;\overline{-}\;\overset{\cup}{}\;\overline{-}\qquad\overline{-}\quad\overset{\cup}{-}\;\;\overset{\cup}{-}\,//$$
sed lŭbet scīre quant(um) aŭr(um) ērus sibi 3 cr ∪ –//

$$\overline{-}\;\overset{\cup}{}\;\overline{-}\quad\overline{-}\;\overset{\cup}{-}/\overline{-}\;\overset{\cup}{-}\;\;\overset{\cup}{}\,\overline{-}\,//$$
dempsit et quid sŭo reddĭdit pătri.   3 cr ∪ –//

Acatalectic cretic dimeters are used primarily as clausulae of cretic systems; e.g., Plautus, *Epidicus* 89: $\overline{-}\;\overset{\cup}{-}\;\overline{-}\overset{\cup}{-}$ *is suo filio*; very rarely cretic dimeters occur in catalectic form, e.g., Plautus, *Truculentus* 123: $\overline{-}\;\overset{\cup}{}\;\overline{-}$ *salva sis.* $-\overline{et\ tu}$.

4. As in Greek poetry, iambs, trochees, bacchiacs, and cretics are often used to complete a sequence of a different character. In the Alcaic strophe, for example (see below, sections XVI and XVIII), iambs are prefixed to Aeolics; in the Sapphic strophe (see below, sections XVI and XVIII), a cretic precedes an Aeolic meter; and in Catullus' favorite, the phalaecean, a bacchiac follows a glyconic. Bacchiacs and iambs are frequently joined together, e.g., Plautus, *Captivi* 507:

$$\overline{-}\quad\overline{-}\overset{\cup}{}\overline{-}\quad\overline{-}\quad\overline{-}\;\overline{-}/\quad\cup\quad\overline{-}\qquad\overline{-}$$
ind(e) īlĭco praevortor dŏmum, postqu(am)

$$\overset{\cup}{}\quad\overline{-}\quad\overline{-}\;\overset{//}{}$$
id āctum (e)st; 2 ia∧/2 ba//

and so are cretics and trochees, e.g., *ibid.* 214:

$$\overline{-}\quad\overset{\cup}{}\quad\overline{-}\;\overline{-}\overset{\cup}{}\overline{-}\quad\overline{-}\;\overset{\cup}{}\;\overline{-}\;\overline{-}\,//$$
sed brĕv(em) ōration(em) incĭpisse. 2 cr tro//

The *lecythion*: $-\cup-\cup-\cup-//$, (notation: lec//), which is the second part of an iambic trimeter taken after the caesura after the second anceps, is used only once by Horace (*Odes* II. 18); he alternates it with catalectic iambic trimeters, see below, section XV. 1. Comedy uses the lecythion also in stichic sequences, permitting the resolution of the first two

longa into two short syllables, and the substitution of a long
or two short syllables for any breve except the last; e.g.,
Plautus, *Epidicus*, 3–6:

$$- \cup \cup\ - -\ \quad - \quad \cup\ \quad\ -\ ^{//}$$
respice vero, Thespri(o). – oh, lec //

$$\cup\ \cup\ \cup\ -\ \quad\ \cup\ \cup\ -\ \quad\ \cup\ -^{//}$$
Epidicumn(e) ego conspicor? — lec //

$$\cup\ \cup\ \quad\ -\ \quad \cup\ \cup - - \cup -^{//}$$
sati(s) rect(e) oculis uteris. — lec//

$$-\ \quad -\ \quad\ -\ \quad -\ \quad\ -\ \cup -^{//}$$
salve. – di dent quae velis. lec//

The *ithyphallic* ($- \cup - \cup - -$, notation: ith/) is the second
half of the catalectic iambic trimeter taken after the caesura
after the second anceps. Horace uses it only once to form an
asynarteton (see below, section XV. 2), the so-called "ar-
chilochean" line, which alternates with a catalectic iambic
trimeter (*Odes* I. 4. 1–2):

$$- \cup \cup - \cup\ \quad \cup -\ \quad - - \cup\cup/-\cup\ -\ \cup\ - -^{//}$$
solvitur acris hiems grata vice veris et Favoni 4 da$\cup\cup$/ith//

$$\cup\ -\ \quad \cup\ -\ -/\ -\ \cup\ -\ \cup - -^{//}$$
trahuntque siccas machinae carinas, . . . 3 ia$_\wedge$//

Note how in the second line the part after the caesura
forms the ithyphallic. In comedy the ithyphallic frequently
serves as the clausula of a cretic system; it is also sometimes
used in conjunction with other verse forms to form asynar-
teta (see below, section XV. 2), e.g., Plautus, *Pseudolus* 1268:

$$- \cup \cup\ \quad \cup\ \quad\ -\ \quad\ \cup -\ \quad \cup \cup\ \quad\ -$$
hoc ego mod(o) atqu(e) erus minor hunc

$$\cup -/\ -\ \quad \cup\ -\ \quad \cup\ - -^{//}$$
diem sumpsimus prothyme, . . . cr gl/ ith//

XIII. Ionics and Choriambs

Latin ionics and choriambs differ from those in Greek in that
they permit, especially in comedy, substitution of a long
syllable for the two brevia and resolution of the long into
two short syllables on a much more liberal scale.

1. (a) Plautus and Terence occasionally employ *choriambic* periods in systems dominated by cretics or Aeolics (for Aeolics see below, section XVI); e.g., Plautus, *Menaechmi* 110:

— ‿‿ — — ‿ ‿—╱   — ‿ ‿
ni mala, ni stulta sies, n(i) indomit(a)
      — ·—   ‿ ‿ —∥
      inposqu(e) animi, ..   4 cho∥

(b) Latin also knows the *polyschematist choriamb*; but it is treated much more freely than it is in Greek. Its chief characteristic is that it always ends in a choriamb which is preceded by four elements. Any of these elements can be long or short or double short, but the four together usually do not form a choriamb: ‿‿ ‿‿ ‿‿ ‿‿ — ‿ ‿—╱ (notation: polysch╱). It also exists in acephalous form. In Plautus, *Menaechmi* 111–114, a polyschematist + acephalous polyschematist is sandwiched between a choriambic tetrameter (line 110, quoted above) and cretic tetrameters, after which follow two polyschematists:

— ‿ —   ‿ ‿— ‿ ‿ —╱—‿ ‿
quod vir(o) ess(e) odio videas, tute tib(i)
     ‿ ‿   ‿ ‿—∥
     odi(o) habeas.   polysch╱ₐpolysch∥
— ‿ — — ‿— —‿ —   — ‿—∥
praeterhac si mihi tale post hunc diem   4 cr∥
— ‿ —— ‿— ‿ ‿‿ —— ‿ — ∥
faxis, faxo foris vidua visas patrem.   4 cr∥
—   ‿‿— ‿ ‿ —‿ ‿—╱ — ‿‿—
nam quotiens foras ire volo, me retines,
     ‿ ‿—   ‿ ‿ —∥
     revocas, rogitas,   2 polysch∥

Choriambs with bacchiac ending occur in later Latin poetry, especially in Ausonius and Martianus Capella, e.g. Ausonius IX. 4. 1:

—‿‿ —   — ‿‿— — ‿ ‿ —╱ ‿— —∥
delicium, blanditiae, ludus, amor, voluptas.   3 cho╱ ba∥

2. (a) A system of pure *ionics*, normally with word ending after each metron, occurs only once in Latin poetry: Horace, *Odes* III. 12 is usually divided into four stanzas of 10 ionics each, e.g., lines 1–3:

$$\cup\cup--\quad\cup\quad\cup--\cup\cup--\quad\cup\ \cup-\bar{}$$
miserarum (e)st nequ(e) amori dare ludum neque dulci

$$\cup\cup--\cup\cup\quad--\cup\cup--\quad\cup\cup--\quad\cup\cup-$$
mala vino laver(e), aut exanimari metuentis patruae

$$-\cup\cup-\ -\ //$$
verbera linguae.

However, ionics with resolutions and substitutions are fairly common, e.g., Plautus, *Pseudolus* 1257 (with iambic shortening, cf. above, section II. 4):

$$-\ -\ -\ \cup\cup\ --/\cup\ \cup\ -\ -\ \cup\cup\ --$$
hic omnes voluptates, in hoc omnes venustates . . . 4 io//

Ionics may also be combined with other meters to form asynarteta (see below, section XV. 2), e.g., with dactyls in Boethius, *De Consolatione Philosophiae* III. 6. 1:

$$-\quad\cup\ \cup\ -\quad\cup\ \cup\ -\ -\ -/\ \cup\ \cup-\ -\cup\ \cup\ --//$$
omn(e) hominum genus in terris simili surgit ab ortu

$$4\ da_\wedge/2\ io//$$

or with trochees, *ibid.*, IV. 2. 1:

$$-\ \cup-\ \cup-\cup\ --/\cup\cup-\ -\cup\ \cup\ --//$$
quos vides sedere celsos solii culmine reges.\qquad 2 tro/2 io//

Ionic tetrameters also exist in acephalous form with the first two elements omitted, e.g., Afranius, line 202 Ribbeck II:

$$-\quad-\ \cup\quad\cup--\quad/\ \cup\cup\ -\ -\cup\ \cup--//$$
mult(a) atque molesta (e)s: potin' ut dicta facessas?

$${}_{\wedge\wedge}4\ io//$$

(b) *Anaclastic ionic dimeters* (notation: anacl/), also called *anacreontics*, are found in their pure form in the poetry of the Empire. They are ionic dimeters in which the fourth and fifth elements are reversed, e.g., Hadrian in *Scriptores Historiae Augustae: Hadrian* 16. 4:

$$\cup\cup \;\; -\cup \;\; -\cup \;\; --$$
ego nolo Florus esse,   anacl/

$$- \;\;\;\; -\cup \;\; - \;\; \cup -- $$
amb(u)lare per tabernas,   2 ia$_\wedge$/

$$\cup\cup -\cup - \;\; \cup --/$$
latitare per popinas,   anacl/

$$\cup\cup - \;\; \cup- \cup - \;\; -//$$
culices pati rotundos.   anacl//

They may be found in the same system with iambs, choriambs, or other meters, e.g., Seneca, *Medea* 849–852:

$$-- \;\;\;\; \cup - \cup \;\; - \;\; -/$$
quonam cruenta maenas   2 ia$_\wedge$/

$$-- \;\;\; \cup \;\; -\cup \;\; --/$$
praeceps amore saevo   2 ia$_\wedge$/

$$\cup\cup - \;\;\;\; \cup \;\; - \;\;\;\; \cup --/$$
rapitur? quod impotenti   anacl/

$$\cup\cup - \;\;\; \cup - \;\; \cup--//$$
facinus parat furore?   anacl//

or Claudian, *Fescennina* 2. 1–4:

$$\cup\cup \;\; - \cup \;\;\;\; - \cup--/$$
age cuncta nuptiali   anacl/

$$\cup\cup \;\; -\cup \;\; -\cup \;\; --/$$
redimita vere tellus   anacl/

$$\cup\cup \;\; - \cup - \cup--/$$
celebra toros eriles;   anacl/

$$- \;\; \cup \;\; \cup \;\; - \;\;\;\; - \;\;\;\; \cup\cup- //$$
omne nemus cum fluviis, . . .   2 cho//

Anaclasis also occurs in acephalous ionic tetrameters. In the following example, a period with one such anaclasis (between the third and fourth metra) alternates with a period that has double anaclasis (between the second and third and the third and fourth metra); the latter gives a trochaic effect: Plautus, *Amphitruo* 168–169:

‒ ‒ ⏑ ⏑‒   ‒ ⏑ ⏑‒ ⏑‒ ⏑ ‒ ‒ (e)st //
noctesque diesqu(e) adsiduo satis superque (e)st
simple anaclasis

‒ ‒   ‒ ‒   ⏑ ‒ ⏑ ‒   ⏑‒⏑ ‒ ‒ //
quod fact(o) aut dict(o) adest opus, quietu(s) ne sis.
double anaclasis

The acephalous tetrameters with simple anaclasis are also known as *sotadeans*, named after the Alexandrian poet Sotades (third century B.C.). They were occasionally used by the poets of the Empire, e.g., Martial III. 29. 1:

‒ ‒   ⏑ ⏑‒ ‒ ⏑ ⏑ ‒⏑ ‒ ⏑ ‒ ‒ //
has cum gemina compede dedicat catenas.

Related to these verse forms is the so-called *galliambic*, which is used only once in Latin literature, viz. by Catullus, no. 63. It is an asynarteton (see below, section XV. 2) which consists of an anaclastic dimeter + a catalectic dimeter (which may or may not have anaclasis) with regular diaeresis between the two. In the second dimeter, the second longum is almost always resolved into two short syllables: lines 1–2:

⏑ ⏑ ‒ ⏑ ‒ ⏑ ‒ ‒ / ⏑ ⏑‒ ⏑ ⏑ ⏑ ⏑‒ //
super alta vectus Attis celeri rate maria,   anacl/ 2 io$_\wedge$//

⏑ ⏑   ‒ ⏑ ‒ ⏑‒ ‒ / ⏑ ⏑‒ ⏑ ⏑
Phrygi(um) ut nemus citato cupide pede
⏑ ⏑‒ //
tetigit, . . .   anacl/ 2 io$_\wedge$//

XIV. *Combinations of Lyric Meters*

The Roman poets, especially Plautus, Catullus, and Horace, also imitated those lyric Greek verse forms which have as their basic units not only the common metra of dactyl, iamb, trochee, ionic (including their derivatives, such as cretic and bacchiac), but also longer structures which cannot be reduced to these common metra. Such verse forms will be discussed in the following sections.

93

XV. Epodes and Asynarteta

Horace is chiefly responsible for having imported into Latin poetry those ingenious combinations of different verse forms that Archilochus had invented (see *Greek Meters*, section 15). But even before Horace some such combinations are found in Plautus; and many of Horace's successors elaborated the forms which Horace had introduced.

1. An *epode* is composed of two different metrical units which may or may not be based upon the same meter. The two units are separated by a pause so as to form a couplet. This kind of verse is best known from the *Epodes* of Horace.

In the most popular form, used by Horace in *Epodes* 1–10, an iambic trimeter is followed by an iambic dimeter, e.g., Horace, *Epodes* 2:

$$\cup - \cup - \cup \, - \, \cup - \, \cup - \cup - /$$
beátus ílle quī prócul negótiīs,   3 ia//

$$- \, - \cup - \, - - \cup - //$$
ut prīscā géns mortálium, . . .   2 ia//

Such couplets are also found in Vergil, *Catalepton* 13; Seneca, *Medea* 771–786; Ausonius, and other poets.

A different form of iambic epode is employed in Horace, *Odes* II. 18:

$$- \cup - \cup \quad - \cup - //$$
non ébur néqu(e) aúreum   lec//

$$\cup - \cup - \cup \, - \cup - - - //$$
meā rénidet in dómo lacúnar, . . .   3 ia∧//

Dactylic epodes, composed of dactylic hexameter + tetrameter, occur in Horace, *Odes* I. 7; I. 28; and in *Epodes* 12:

$$- \cup\cup - \quad \cup\cup - / - - \, - \, - \cup \cup - - //$$
quid tíbi vīs, múlier nígris digníssima bárris?   6 da∧//

$$- \cup\cup \quad - \quad \cup\cup \quad - \cup \cup - - //$$
múnera quíd mihi quídve tabéllas. . . .   4 da⁻//

In *Odes* IV. 7, a dactylic hexameter is followed by a hemiepes:

94

$$— — — \cup \; \cup — / \; \cup \; \cup — \quad — \quad — \cup \cup \; — \; —//$$
diffugere nives, redeunt iam gramina campis   6 da$_\wedge$//

$$— \cup \cup — \; \cup \; \cup —//$$
arboribusque comae; . . . .   3 da$_{\wedge\wedge}$//

Dactylic hexameters are also found with iambic dimeters or trimeters, e.g., Horace, *Epodes* 14:

$$— \cup \; \cup — \cup \cup — \; — — / — — \cup \cup — —//$$
mollis inertia cur tantam diffuderit imis   6 da$_\wedge$//

$$— — \cup — — \; — \cup —//$$
oblivionem sensibus, ...   2 ia//

or *Epodes* 16:

$$— \cup \cup \; — \; \cup \cup —/ — — \; — — \cup \cup \; — \; —//$$
altera iam teritur bellis civilibus aetas,   6 da$_\wedge$//

$$\cup — \cup — \; \cup / \; — \cup \; — \cup — \; \cup —//$$
suis et ipsa Roma viribus ruit.   3 ia//

Ausonius was the chief imitator of Horace in the use of this verse form.

2. An *asynarteton* is a verse composed of two different metrical units that follow one another without pause, but have diaeresis between the two units.

The so-called *archilochean* line, consisting of 4 da$^{\cup\cup}$/ith// has been cited in section XII. 4, above. Horace, *Odes* I. 4. 1 (see also 3, below):

$$— \cup \cup — \cup \; \cup — \quad — — \; \cup \cup / — \cup \; — \; \cup \; — —//$$
solvitur acris hiems grata vice veris et Favoni. . . .

4 da$^{\cup\cup}$/ith//

While Horace uses the archilochean only once as part of an expanded epode (see below, 3), later poets used it also for stichic compositions, e.g. Boethius, *De Consolatione Philosophiae* V. 5. 1–2:

$$— \quad \cup \cup — \; — — \; \cup \cup \; —\cup\cup/ — \; \cup — \; \cup — —//$$
quam variis terras animalia permeant figuris: 4 da$^{\cup\cup}$/ith//

$$— \quad \cup \cup \quad — — \; — — \quad — \; \cup \cup/$$
namqu(e) ali(a) extento sunt corpore

$$— \; \cup \; — \quad \cup \; — \; —//$$
pulveremque verrunt.   4 da$^{\cup\cup}$/ith//

Elsewhere Horace combines dactyls and iambs into asynarteta. Thus we get the *elegiambic*, which consists of a hemiepes and an iambic dimeter. E.g. Horace, *Epodes* 11. 2 (see also 3, below):

$$\overline{}\cup\cup\ \overline{}\cup\cup\ \overline{}/\cup\ \overline{}\ \cup\ \overline{}\ \overline{}\ \overline{}\ \cup\ \overline{}//$$

scribere versiculos amore percussum gravi,   3 da$_{\wedge\wedge}$/2 ia//

and its reverse, the *iambelegiac*, in which the iambic dimeter precedes the hemiepes, e.g. Horace, *Epodes* 13. 4 (see also 3, below):

$$\overline{}\ \overline{}\cup\overline{}\ \overline{}\ \overline{}\ \cup\overline{}/\ \overline{}\ \cup\ \cup\overline{}\ \cup\ \cup\overline{}//$$

occasionem de die, dumque virent genua.   2 ia/3 da$_{\wedge\wedge}$//

Asynarteta may also be composed of two different units based on the same meter. The *diphilean* verse is made up of a hemiepes followed by a prosodiac ($\times - \cup\cup - \cup\cup -/$; notation: enop$_{\wedge}$/)*, e.g. Plautus, *Casina* 644:

$$\overline{}\ \cup\ \cup\ \overline{}\ \cup\cup\ \overline{}\ \overline{}\ \overline{}\cup\cup\ \overline{}\ \cup\ \cup\ \overline{}//$$

iam tib(i) istuc cerebrum dispercuti(am),   excetra tu.

3 da$_{\wedge\wedge}$/enop$_{\wedge}$//

Boethius, *De Consolatione Philosophiae* I. 2, combines the hemiepes with the last two metra of a dactylic hexameter (= adonic):

$$\overline{}\ \overline{}\ \overline{}\cup\cup\overline{}/\ \overline{}\cup\ \cup\overline{}\ \overline{}//$$

heu quam praecipiti mersa profundo.   3 da$_{\wedge\wedge}$/adon//

Of the many other combinations that make up asynarteta, we shall here only mention the *priapean*, named after the fertility god Priapus and consisting of glyconic + pherecratean (for these Aeolic meters, see below, section XVI). E.g. Catullus, no. 17. 1:

$$\overline{}\ \cup\overline{}\cup\cup\ \overline{}\ \cup\overline{}/\ \overline{}\ \cup\ \overline{}\ \cup\cup\ \overline{}\ \overline{}//$$

o Colonia, quae cupis ponte ludere longo.   gl/ ph//

* The prosodiac is best explained as a catalectic enoplion. For the enoplion see *Greek Meters*, section 15.

3. There exists also a kind of *expanded epode*, in which an asynarteton forms one of the periods.

Horace, *Odes* I. 4 joins a catalectic iambic trimeter to an archilochean (lines 1–2):

$$— \cup\cup —\cup \;\; \cup— \quad\; —— \cup\cup/—\cup — \;\cup ——//$$
solvitur acris hiems grata vice veris et Favoni
$$4da^{\cup\cup}/\text{ith}//$$

$$\cup — \;\; \cup —— \;\; —\cup — \;\cup——//$$
trahuntque siccas machinae carinas. $\qquad$ 3 ia$_\wedge$//

In *Epodes* 11 an iambic trimeter precedes an elegiambic (lines 1–2):

$$—— \;\; \cup— \;\; —/—\cup — \;\cup—\cup —//$$
Petti, nihil me sicut antea iuvat $\qquad$ 3 ia//

$$— \cup\cup \; — \cup\cup—/\cup —\cup \;\; —— \; — \;\; \cup—//$$
scribere versiculos amore percussum gravi, $\qquad$ 3 da$_{\wedge\wedge}$/2 ia//

and in *Epodes* 13 a dactylic hexameter is followed by an iambelegiac (lines 1–2):

$$— \cup\cup \;\; — \;\; ——/ \;\; — \;\; — \;\; — \;\; —\cup \cup \;\; — \;\; —//$$
horrida tempestas caelum contraxit et imbres $\quad$ 6 da$_\wedge$//

$$\cup — \;\; \cup \;\; ——— \quad \cup \;\; —/ \;\; — \quad \cup \cup \;\; — \quad \cup\cup—//$$
nivesque deducunt Iovem; nunc mare, nunc siluae
$$\text{2 ia/3 da}_{\wedge\wedge}//$$

XVI. Aeolic Meters

Horace's claim (*Odes* III. 30. 13–14) *"princeps Aeolium carmen ad Italos// deduxisse modos"* is justified to the extent that he was the first Roman to imitate the Aeolics of Greek poetry on a large scale. Before Horace, Catullus had experimented with some Aeolic verse forms, and others appear in the *cantica* of Plautus' comedies. For the chief Aeolic meters, see above, section I.

Plautus treats the glyconic with the same kind of freedom with which he treats most Greek meters: two brevia may take the place of one of the two ancipitia or of the breve before the last longum. Catullus, and also Seneca, follow the Greek patterns fairly closely, but occasionally permit a long syllable to take the place of the two brevia in the "choriambic" nucleus.

But it is Horace whose practices standardized Latin Aeolics. In his Aeolic verses as well as those of most of his successors the ancipitia of the Aeolic base regularly become longa. Moreover, as stated in section IX, above, the caesurae which appear only occasionally in the Aeolics of Catullus become a regular phenomenon in Horace, as a result of tendencies which developed in the Hellenistic period. The use of the caesura and the avoidance of monosyllables in certain parts of the verse seem to follow principles of word grouping, which originated with the Latin hexameter. The exact nature of these principles has not yet been sufficiently explored, but the spoken hexameter evidently did play a part in forming the spoken Aeolic structures of Horace.

As in Greek, Latin Aeolics appear (1) in simple, i.e. uncompounded, form; or (2) externally or internally compounded.

1. In Latin poetry, only glyconics and pherecrateans appear in their *simple* form. Glyconics in Plautus, *Persa* 268:

$$\overline{-}\,\overline{-}\ -\ \smile\ \smile\ -\,\overline{\smile}\,\text{-}//$$
$$\text{virtus est, ub(i) occasio} \qquad\qquad \text{gl}//$$

or *Bacchides* 990:

$$\smile\ \smile\ \smile\ -\quad\ \smile\ \smile\ -\quad\ \smile\ \smile-//$$
$$\text{tamen ades. - quid opust? - taceas:} \ldots \quad \text{gl}//$$

Stichic compositions in glyconics are found in late writers, such as Seneca, Prudentius, and Boethius; usually, however, a sequence of glyconics includes a pherecratean line, most commonly as a clausula, e.g., Catullus, no. 34. 1–4:

$$\cup- \: - \: \cup \: \cup \: - \: \cup -/$$
Dīanae sūmŭs ĭn fīdĕ   gl/

$$\cup- \: - \: \cup\cup \: - \: \cup \: -//$$
puell(ae) et pŭer(ĭ) integri: gl//

$$\cup- \: - \: \cup\cup \: - \: \cup \: -/$$
Dīanam pŭer(ĭ) integri   gl/

$$\cup- \: - \: \cup \: \cup \: - \: -///$$
puellaeque canamus.   ph///

A glyconic followed by a pherecratean forms the *priapean* asynarteton, see above, section XV. 2.

2. The variety of *compounded* Aeolics is as great in Latin as it is in Greek. (a) *Internal compounding* takes place when the "dactyl" or the "choriamb" of the Aeolic verse is repeated *within* the Aeolic unit. For example, the *asclepiadean* verse is a glyconic internally compounded by repeating the "choriamb" (notation: gl^c//), e.g., Horace, *Odes* I. 1. 1:

$$- \: --\: \cup\cup \: -/-\cup\cup \: - \: \cup \: -//$$
Maecenas atavis edite regibus.   gl^c//

Note that in Horace and his successors caesura always occurs after the first "choriamb" (the only exceptions are: *Odes* II. 12. 25 and IV. 8. 17). Horace uses this verse form in stichic sequence (as did Seneca, Prudentius, and others) and in various combinations with glyconics and pherecrateans, see below, section XVIII.

The "choriamb" may be repeated twice (*major asclepiadean*; notation: gl^2c//). While Horace (*Odes* I. 11; 18; IV. 10) and Catullus (no. 30) use this verse only for stichic compositions, Prudentius combines it with gl^c//. E.g., Horace, *Odes* I. 18. 1:

$$- \: - \: -\cup \: \cup \: -/-\cup \: \cup-/-\cup\cup \: - \: \cup \: -//$$
Nullam, Vare, sacra vite prius severis arborem.   gl^2c//

Note the two caesurae, which regularly mark off the second "choriamb".

(b) In *external compounding* one or two non-Aeolic elements, usually iambs, cretics, or bacchiacs, are prefixed or subjoined to the Aeolic verse. One of Catullus' favorite meters consists of a glyconic to which a bacchiac is added (*phalaecean* or *hendecasyllabic*: ×× − ∪∪ − ∪ − ∪ − − //; notation: gl ba//). E.g., Catullus, no. 1. 1–2:

$$- \ -- \ \cup\cup \ - \ \cup \ - \ \cup -- \ //$$
cui dono lepidum novum libellum   gl ba//

$$-\cup- \ \cup\cup \ - \ \cup \ - \ \cup-- \ //$$
arida modo pumic(e) expolitum?   gl ba//

There is a tendency, but no necessity, to have a caesura after the "choriamb" or after the brevia of the "choriamb". Catullus uses gl ba// only in stichic compositions.

In the *sapphic* verse, a cretic precedes an acephalous hipponactean (− ∪ − × − ∪∪ − ∪ − −, notation: cr ∧hipp//). Though Catullus follows the Greek models in permitting either a long or a short syllable at the anceps and in avoiding a regular caesura, more than half of his sapphics have word ending after the fifth syllable. Caesura after the fifth syllable then became regular with and after Horace (except for the *Carmen Saeculare* and *Odes* IV, where it often occurs after the sixth syllable) and the anceps became regularly long. E.g., Horace, *Odes* I. 22. 1–2:

$$- \cup \ - \ --/ \ \cup\cup \ - \ \cup \ --//$$
integer vitae scelerisque purus   cr ∧hipp//

$$- \ \cup \ - \ --/ \ \cup \ \cup- \ \cup \ --//$$
non eget Mauris iaculis nequ(e) arcu. . . .   cr ∧hipp//

An interesting by-product of the caesura after the fifth syllable and the long anceps is that the word accent in the first part of a sapphic verse regularly – though not invariably – falls on the first and fourth syllables. What is cause and what effect is hard to determine: did a consideration of word accent regularize the caesura, or did the caesura, which must have developed with the use of originally sung meters for spoken verse, determine the incidence of word accent? The fact that the incidence of word accent on long element is less regular in sapphics than it is in alcaics suggests that word accent was not the primary consideration; yet there is no reason why Horace should not have availed himself of the word accent given him by his language in some way to naturalize sapphics into Latin.

The sapphic occurs almost exclusively as a component of the Sapphic strophe (see below, section XVIII), but there are examples of stichic sapphics in Seneca and Boethius.

In addition, Horace (*Odes* I. 8) once employs an acephalous hipponactean compounded not only externally by a cretic, but also internally by a choriamb (= *major sapphic*). Caesura after the first "choriamb" is the rule. The verse appears in an epode alternating with cho ba/ (= *aristophanean*). E.g., Horace, *Odes* I. 8. 13–14:

$$\overline{} \cup \cup \; — \; \cup \overline{} \; —/$$
quid latet, ut marinae   cho ba/

$$—\cup— \;\; —— \;\; \cup\cup—/— \; \cup \; \cup \; —\cup \;\; ——/\!/$$
filium dicunt Thetidis sub lacrimosa Troiae   cr ˌhipp^e/$\!$/

When an acephalous glyconic is preceded by an iambic metron, the result is the *alcaic hendecasyllable* ($×—\cup—\overline{×}$ $—\cup\cup—\cup—/\!/$, notation: ia ˌgl/$\!$/), which constitutes each of the first two periods of the Alcaic strophe (see below, section XVIII). The place of the second anceps is always taken by a long syllable, and there is always caesura after it. E.g., Horace, *Odes* II. 3. 1–2:

$$\overline{} \quad — \quad \cup \; —— / \; — \cup \; \cup \; — \; \cup\overline{} \; /\!/$$
aequam memento rebus in arduis   ia ˌgl/$\!$/

$$——\cup \; — \; —/ \; — \; \cup\cup \; — \; \cup\overline{} \; /\!$$
servare mentem, non secus in bonis. . . . ia ˌgl/$\!$/

It is noteworthy that in the alcaic hendecasyllable the natural word accent falls generally on the 1st, 4th, 6th, and 9th syllables. Some later poets, e.g., Claudian, Prudentius, and Ennodius, use this verse for stichic compositions.

It remains to say a few words about the forms which the acephalous pherecratean or "reizianum" (× — ◡ ◡ — —/; notation: ₐph/) adopts in Plautus. It admits of great variety (◡̆◡̆ ◡◡ ◡̆◡̆ ◡◡ ——/) and is frequently found in combination with iambs, anapaests, cretics, and glyconics. Although here, too, we do not know exactly how the Romans recognized its rhythm, they may have been helped by the fact that the word accent usually falls on the first (or second) and the next-to-last syllable. In the following example, taken from a long passage in Plautus, *Aulularia* 415–445, iambic dimeters precede acephalous pherecrateans; ibid. 415–416:

◡ ◡   — ◡ —   —   ◡ ◡   ◡ —/   —
redi. quo fugis nunc? tene, tene. – quid,

◡ ◡ ◡   —   — //
stolide, clamas? –   ia⁴/ ₐph//

◡   ◡   — ◡ —   ◡ ◡ — ◡ — /
qui(a) ad trisviros i(am) ego deferam

— —   ◡ ◡   —   — //
nomen tuom. – qu(am) ob rem?   ia⁴/ ₐph//

XVII. Stichic and non-stichic Lyric Poetry

We have been concerned in sections X–XVI with the various meters in which Latin lyrics are composed. Many of these meters, as we saw, are used in stichic compositions: Catullus, no. 4, and Horace, *Epode* 17, for example, consist entirely of iambic trimeters (see section XII. 1), Horace, *Odes* III. 12 of ionics, and Catullus, no. 63, of galliambics (see section XIII. 2 (b)). Of the Aeolic meters (section XVI) asclepiadeans (gl^c//) appear in stichic sequence in Horace, *Odes* I. 1; III. 30; and IV. 8, and major asclepiadeans (gl²ᶜ//) in Catullus, no. 30, and Horace, *Odes* I. 11; 18; and IV. 10. Furthermore, Catullus' favorites are stichic phalaeceans (gl ba//) and iambic trimeters with a longum in place of the last breve (choliambs).

In addition to these, we have had occasion to discuss, in section XV, the structure of most of Horace's *Epodes* and those of his *Odes* which are composed in the form of epodes; in section XVI. 1, brief mention was made of that rather popular strophe in which a number of glyconics, usually three, are rounded off by a pherecratean clausula.

But while Catullus generally prefers to compose lyrics in stichic sequence, most of Horace's poems combine a number of different periods to form a strophe, and the same is true to a large extent of the *cantica* of drama. Accordingly, the next section (XVIII) will deal with the structure of the non-stichic poems of Horace, and section XIX with the *cantica* of Plautus and Seneca.

XVIII. The Odes of Horace

Most modern printed editions of Horace arrange each poem in the four books of *Odes* into strophes of four lines each. This arrangement is due to the discovery of the German scholar August Meineke that the number of lines in each ode is divisible by four. *Odes* IV. 8, which consists of 34 asclepiadeans and is, accordingly, not divisible by four, becomes a four-line scheme by excising two spurious lines (17 and 33). Although the four-line strophe is well suited to a pattern such as the statement-and-response of *Odes* III. 9, there are several reasons for rejecting the view that Horace used it as a deliberate and consistent pattern in all his odes: (a) the "irregularity" of *Odes* IV. 8 has already been mentioned;(b) more often than not a four-line strophe leaves the thought as well as the grammatical structure uncompleted; and (c) Meineke's Law rests on the assumption that Horace considered the Sapphic and Alcaic strophes (see below) as consisting invariably of four periods each. But, though he seems indeed to have done so most of the time, a number of instances make it clear that he could also think of them as three-line compositions. In other words, at best we can speak of a tendency, but not of a necessity, toward a four-line strophe in the *Odes* of Horace.

Horace was especially fond of combining two or more Aeolic verses, usually asclepiadeans, glyconics, and pherecrateans (see section XVI) into the structure of a poem. In the *Second Asclepiadean*,* all the odd lines are glyconic and all the even lines asclepiadean (gl^c//), e.g., *Odes* III. 9. 1–4:

$$\overline{}\ \overline{}\quad \overline{}\cup\ \cup\ \overline{}\ \cup\overline{}//$$
donec gratus eram tibi,   gl//

$$\overline{}\quad \overline{}\ \cup\cup\overline{}/\ \overline{}\ \cup\cup\ \overline{}\ \cup\ \overline{}//$$
nec quisquam potior bracchia candidae gl^c//

$$\overline{}\ \overline{}\ \cup\ \cup\ \overline{}\ \cup\ \overline{}//$$
cervici iuvenis dabat,   gl//

$$\overline{}\ \overline{}\ \overline{}\quad \cup\ \cup\overline{}/\ \overline{}\cup\ \cup\ \overline{}\cup\overline{}\ ///$$
Persarum vigui rege beatior.   gl^c///

In other poems, three asclepiadeans are followed by a glyconic clausula to form the *Third Asclepiadean*, e.g., *Odes* IV. 5. 1–4:

$$\overline{}\ \overline{}\ \cup\ \cup\ \overline{}/\ \overline{}\ \cup\ \cup\ \overline{}\ \cup\ \overline{}//$$
divis orte bonis, optume Romulae   gl^c//

$$\overline{}\ \overline{}\quad \overline{}\cup\ \cup\ \overline{}/\overline{}\ \cup\ \cup\overline{}\ \cup\overline{}//$$
custos gentis, abes iam nimium diu: gl^c//

$$\overline{}\ \overline{}\ \overline{}\quad \cup\cup\ \overline{}/\ \overline{}\cup\cup\overline{}\ \cup\ \overline{}//$$
maturum reditum pollicitus patrum   gl^c//

$$\overline{}\ \overline{}\ \overline{}\ \cup\cup\overline{}\ \cup\ \overline{}///$$
sancto concilio, redi.   gl///

The *Fourth Asclepiadean* consists of two asclepiadeans, a pherecratean, and a glyconic clausula, e.g., *Odes* I. 5. 1–4:

$$\overline{}\quad \overline{}\ \overline{}\quad \cup\cup\overline{}/\ \overline{}\ \cup\cup\ \overline{}\ \cup\overline{}//$$
quis multa gracilis te puer in rosa   gl^c//

* Different scholars use different names for the various systems of Horace. We follow the practice of the most accessible English editions.

⏤⏤⏤ ⏑ ⏑⏤/⏤ ⏑ ⏑ ⏤⏑ ⏤//
perfusus liquidis urget odoribus   gl^c//

⏤⏤ ⏤ ⏑ ⏑ ⏤ ⏤//
grato, Pyrrha, sub antro?   ph//

⏤ ⏤⏤⏤ ⏑⏑⏤ ⏑ ⏤ ///
cui flavam religas comam. . .   gl///

One of the most popular of Horace's verse forms is the Sapphic strophe, in which two sapphics (see section XVI. 2(b)) are followed by cretic + acephalous glyconic + acephalous pherecratean, e.g., *Odes* I. 2. 17–20:

⏤⏑⏤ ⏤ ⏤/⏑ ⏑⏤ ⏑⏤⏤//
Iliae dum se nimium querenti   cr ˌhipp//

⏤ ⏑ ⏤ ⏤ ⏤/ ⏑ ⏑ ⏤ ⏑⏤ ⏤//
iactat ultorem, vagus et sinistra   cr ˌhipp//

⏤⏑⏤ ⏤⏤/⏑ ⏑ ⏤ ⏑ ⏤ ⏤ ⏤⏑⏑ ⏤ ⏤ ///
labitur ripa Iove non probant(e) uxorius amnis.   cr ˌgl ˌph///

However, since in the third line word ending usually occurs after the anceps of ˌph, and since at the same place a hiatus is found twice (*Odes* I. 2. 47 and I. 22. 15), Horace may have considered the Sapphic strophe as consisting of three sapphic lines followed by the last two metra of the dactylic hexameter (= adonic). Catullus employs this verse form only twice.

The *Greater Sapphic* epode, used only once by Horace (*Odes* I. 8), consists of cho ba// (aristophaneans) in the odd and cr ˌhipp^c// (major sapphics) in the even lines, e.g., *Odes* I. 8. 13–16:

⏤ ⏑⏑ ⏤ ⏑⏤ ⏤//
quid latet, ut marinae   cho ba//

⏤⏑⏤ ⏤ ⏤ ⏑⏑⏤/⏤ ⏑ ⏑ ⏤⏑
filium dicunt Thetidis sub lacrimosa

⏤⏤ //
Troiae   cr ˌhipp^c//

⏤ ⏑⏑ ⏤ ⏑⏤ ⏤ //
funera, ne virilis   cho ba//

⏤ ⏑ ⏤ ⏤ ⏤ ⏑ ⏑⏤/ ⏤⏑⏑⏤
cultus in caed(em) et Lycias proriperet

⏑ ⏤ ⏤ //
catervas?   cr ˌhipp^c//

Finally, there is the *Alcaic* strophe. It is composed of two alcaic hendecasyllables (ia $_\wedge$gl//) followed by two iambic metra and an acephalous hipponactean internally compounded with a dactyl (2 ia $_\wedge$hipp^d//). That the 2 ia $_\wedge$hipp^d// was originally conceived as one period is indicated by the fact that it forms one unit in Horace, *Odes* II. 3. 27 and III. 29. 35. However, hiatus between the anceps and the first "dactyl" of hipp^d is so common that it is clear that Horace preferred to divide this unit into two lines, consisting of nine and ten syllables respectively. Accordingly, the third line of the Horatian Alcaic strophe may be regarded as consisting of an iamb + penthemimer ($\times - \cup - \times =$ iambic trimeter taken to its most common caesura after the second anceps; notation: penthem); and the fourth line as hemiepes + bacchiac. E.g. *Odes* II. 14. 1–4:

$$- \ - \ \cup \ - - / \ - \ \cup \ \cup \ - \ \cup \ -//$$
eheu fugaces, Postume, Postume,   ia $_\wedge$gl//

$$- \ - \ \cup \ - \ -/ - \ \cup\cup - \ \ \cup \ -//$$
labuntur anni nec pietas moram   ia $_\wedge$gl//

$$- - \ \ \cup - \ \ - - \cup - \ -/$$
rugis et instanti senectae   ia penthem/

$$- \ \cup\cup - \ \ \cup \ \cup - \ \ \cup \ \ - \ -///$$
adferet indomitaeque morti, ... 3 da$_{\wedge\wedge}$ ba///

XIX. The Cantica of Plautus and Seneca

A few general remarks on the *cantica* of Plautus and Seneca have been made in sections VII and IX, above. The fact that Plautus modelled his *cantica* on Greek drama but has no choral lyrics, while Seneca imitated the lyric meters used by Horace for choral compositions, makes it more convenient to treat the two dramatists separately. It should, however, be stated at the outset that the variety of composition in the *cantica* of both Plautus and Seneca is so great that we cannot here give more than a general outline of the most common structural patterns.

1. The *cantica* of Plautus are most easily divided into (a) those in which a given verse form dominates or is used exclusively, and (b) those in which two or more verse forms are mixed together in the different periods. In either case, the strophic responsion of Greek dramatic lyrics is almost totally absent in Plautus.

(a) Anapaestic *cantica*, consisting entirely of dimeters and/ or tetrameters, the latter in both acatalectic and catalectic form (see above, section XI), occur in *Aulularia* 713–726; *Bacchides* 1076–1108, 1149–1206; *Cistellaria* 203–229; *Persa* 168–180; *Pseudolus* 230–242; *Rudens* 220–228; *Stichus* 309–329; *Trinummus* 256–300, 820–842; etc.

Pure trochaic and iambic sequences are practically nonexistent in the *cantica* of Plautus. Terence, however, occasionally employs them for recitative portions. That means that they are modelled on spoken rather than on sung verse, and that the structural unit is the foot rather than the metron. They are usually built in a pattern in which one trochaic septenarius is sandwiched between a number of trochaic octonarii and iambic octonarii. E.g., Terence, *Eunuchus* 615–617:

ita me di ament, quant(um) eg(o) illum vidi,

    non nil timeo misera,   tro^8 ||

nequ(am) ill(e) hodi(e) insanu(s) turbam

    faciat aut vim Thaidi.   tro^7 ||

nam postqu(am) ist(e) advenit Chremes

    adulescens, frater virginis. . . .   ia^8 ||

However, Plautus was particularly fond of long cretic and bacchiac sequences, which are extremely rare in the extant Greek dramatic lyrics, and we often find iambic and trochaic

elements mixed in with them. Examples of pure cretics and
bacchiacs have been quoted in section XII. 3, above. The
following two passages are intended to convey some idea of
the ways in which predominantly cretic and bacchiac pas-
sages can have an admixture of iambs and trochees.

Plautus, *Amphitruo* 219–226:

$$\text{postqu(am)}\ \overset{\smile}{\text{utrimqu(e)}}\ \overset{-\smile\ -}{\text{exitum}}\ \overset{/}{\text{(e)st}}$$

$$\overset{-\ \smile\ -\ -\smile-//}{\text{maxuma copia,.}}\quad 4\ cr//$$

220 $$\overset{-\ -\ --\ \smile-/-\ --\ -\ \smile-//}{\text{dispertiti viri, dispertit(i) ordines,}}\quad 4\ cr//$$

$$\overset{-\ -\ -\ -\smile\ -\ -\ \smile}{\text{nos nostras more nostr(o) et mod(o)}}$$

$$\overset{-\ -\smile\ -//}{\text{instruximus}}\quad 4\ cr//$$

$$\overset{\smile\smile--\ \smile\ \ --\ -\ \ -\ \smile\smile--}{\text{legiones, it(em) hostes contra legiones}}$$

$$\overset{\frown\ -\ \ \smile\ -\ ///}{\text{suas instruont.}}\quad tro^7$$
$$(=3\ tro\ cr)///$$

$$\overset{\frown\ -\ \smile\ -\ \ -\ \smile\ ----}{\text{deind(e) utriqu(e) imperatores in}}$$

$$\overset{\smile\smile\ \ -\smile-//}{\text{medi(um) exeunt,}}\quad 2\ cr\ lec//$$

$$\overset{-\ -\ -\ \ -\ \smile\ -/-\ \smile\ -\ -}{\text{extra turb(am) ordinum conloquontur}}$$

$$\overset{\smile\ -//}{\text{simul.}}\quad 4\ cr//$$

225 $$\overset{-\ \smile-\ -\ \ \smile-/-\ \smile-\ -\smile-//}{\text{convenit, vict(i) utri sint eo proelio,}}\quad 4\ cr//$$

$$\overset{-\ \ \smile\ \ --\ \smile-/-\ \ \smile-}{\text{urb(em), agr(um), aras, focos sequ(e) uti}}$$

$$\overset{-\smile-//}{\text{dederent.}}\quad 4\ cr//$$

Cretic tetrameters dominate the sequence, which is inter-
rupted by two lines in related meters: both lines 222 and 223
end in a cretic, and line 223 begins with two cretics. How-
ever, the final cretic of line 222 is better interpreted as be-
longing to a trochaic septenarius, while the final cretic of line
223 is perhaps best taken as the end of a lecythion.

Some of the different ways in which bacchiacs may be used are illustrated by Plautus, *Casina* 684–695, which is part of a longer passage (648–705) written predominantly in bacchiacs:

neque (e)st neque fuit me senex

quisqu(am) amator   4 ba//

685 adaeque miser. — lud(o) eg(o) hunc facete;

2 ba penthem//

nam quae facta dix(i) omni(a) huic falsa

dixi: 4 ba//

er(a) atqu(e) haec dol(um) ex proxum(o)

hunc protulerunt,   4 ba//

eg(o) hunc missa sum luder(e). — heus

Pardalisca!   4 ba//

— quid est? — est — quid? — est quod

vol(o) exquirer(e) ex te.   4 ba//

690 — mor(am) offers mih(i). — at tu mih(i)

offers maerorem.   4 ba//

sed etiamn(e) habet nunc Casina

gladium?   2ba/ia²//

— habet, sed duos. — quid, duos? —

altero te   4 ba//

occisur(um) ait, altero vilic(um) hodie.   hipp ba//

— occisissumus s(um) omnium qui vivont.   4 ba//

$$- - \quad\quad - \smile - \quad\quad - \smile \quad\quad - \quad \smile - - \; //$$
695   loric(am) induam m(i) optum(um) ess(e) opinor.

2 ba/penthem//

Bacchiac tetrameters dominate, but they are interspersed with two bacchiacs + penthemimer (lines 685 and 695), a period which ends in a bacchiac; with two bacchiacs + two iambs (line 691), a meter that is rhythmically closely related to the bacchiac; with a bacchiac preceded by a hipponactean (line 693), a period containing anapaestic and bacchiac rhythms; and a catalectic bacchiac tetrameter (line 694).

(b) We cannot even begin to cover the immense variety of ways in which different units are mixed together to form the so-called *mutatis modis cantica*. The following is intended merely as a sample passage to show the kind of combinations that can be found.

Plautus, *Rudens* 185-196 (our line division differs from that in the Oxford text in lines 188–190):

$$\smile\smile \quad \smile\smile \quad - - - - \quad \smile -/$$
185   nimi(o) hominum fortunae minus

$$\smile\smile - \quad \smile \quad \smile - \quad - \; //$$
     miserae memorantur   ia⁴/ ₐph//

$$\smile - \quad - \smile \cap \quad -/-$$
qu(am) in us(u), experiundo is

$$\smile\smile \quad \smile - - \; //$$
    datur acerbum.   2 ba/ ₐph//

$$\smile\smile \quad - \quad \cap - \quad \smile\smile - \quad /$$
⟨satin⟩ hoc deo complacitumst,

$$- - - - \quad - - \quad /$$
   med hoc ornat(u) ornat(am) io cho/ 2{io / cho}/

$$\smile\smile - - \quad \smile\smile - - \quad \smile\smile$$
188-9 in incertas regiones timid(am)

$$- - \quad - \smile \quad \smile \quad -$$
   eiect(am) ? hancin(e) eg(o) ad

$$- \quad - - \quad /$$
      rem natam   3 io cho{io / cho}/

189–90   miserăm mē mĕmŏrāb(o) ?

hancĭn(e) ĕgō partem căpĭ(o)

ŏb pĭĕtātem praecipuam?   3 io cho io cho//

n(am) hōc mī sat lăbōrist

lăbōr(em) hunc pŏtīrī,   4 ba//

sī ergā părent(em) aut dĕōs m(e)

inpĭāvī;   4 ba//

sĕd id sī părătĕ cūrāvī ut cāvĕrem,   4 ba//

tum hōc m(i) indĕcŏre, inīqu(e),

inmŏdestĕ   4 ba//

195   dătĭ(s) dī; nam quĭd hăbēbunt

sĭbī sign(i) inpĭī posthăc,   2 io ia⁴//

s(i) ad hunc mŏdum (e)st innŏxiīs

hŏnŏr ăpŭd vōs ?   /ia⁶//

The passage begins and ends with an iambic rhythm, but between beginning and end we find a number of other rhythms: acephalous pherecratics, choriambs, ionics, and bacchiacs. What all these rhythms have in common is that they "rise", i.e., the breve or brevia precede the longa. Moreover, all these rhythms, except for the iambs and choriambs, rise into two longa, and even the iambs of line 196 conform to the general pattern whereby every line except 190 ends in two long syllables.

But apart from this natural relation among the rhythms

used, it is interesting to observe how one rhythm almost imperceptibly merges into another. The way in which this is done is called *sliding transition* (cf. *Greek Meters*, section 18). The acephalous pherecrateans in lines 185 and 186 end in an "ionic", thus heralding the prominent part played by ionics in lines 187–190. In fact, if one takes the last syllable of *minus* in line 185 as short, it is possible to read the line as a resolved ionic trimeter. Similarly, the bacchiacs which take the place of the iambs in line 186 anticipate the bacchiac tetrameters of lines 191–194.

The next few lines (187–190) are dominated by an ionic-choriambic rhythm. Line 187 starts out by stating all the themes to be struck in this sequence, beginning with an ionic, followed by a choriamb + two metra of three long syllables each (= 2 molossi), which can be interpreted as either choriambs or ionics. Next, after three pure ionics, a choriamb leads into an ambivalent metron of three long syllables (188–189), and finally in the next line (189–190) three ionics are prefixed to two choriambs connected by an ionic.

In order to lead over from ionic-choriamb to bacchiac, the first metra of lines 191 and 192 consist of three longa, which preserve the ionic-choriambic rhythm of the preceding; but with them the bacchiac rhythm is entrenched, and lines 193–194 are composed entirely of bacchiacs.

The last two lines provide the summary of the whole: line 195 begins with two ionics, but adds to them four iambic feet; this leads over into the iambs of line 196, which are

$$\cup \cup \ \cup \cup \ -$$

constructed in such a fashion that the end: *honor apud vos* again recalls the ionics.

2. The *cantica* of Seneca's tragedies, for all their difference from those of Plautus, can also be divided into (a) those

which retain the same rhythm throughout and (b) those composed of more than one basic rhythm. In either case, there is no regular strophic responsion, as there is in Greek dramatic lyrics.

(a) The songs composed in the same rhythm are constructed in a much stricter way than those of Plautus. For example, *Thyestes* 122–175 consists entirely of asclepiadeans (gl^c//), 336–403 entirely of glyconics; *Agamemno* 759–774 entirely of iambic dimeters; etc. Such sequences are occasionally interrupted or concluded by a clausula which consists of the same meter in shortened form: the asclepiadeans of *Troades* 371–407 are rounded out (line 408) by a hemiepes in the form in which it constitutes the first part of the asclepiadean before the caesura. Similarly, the last two metra of the dactylic hexameter (= adonic) interrupt (e.g., *Troades* 825, 835, 850) or conclude (e.g., *Thyestes* 622) a long sequence of sapphics (cr ˄hipp//). Sometimes different stichic systems follow one another: *Medea* 56–74 is composed of asclepiadeans, 75–92 of glyconics, 93–109 again of asclepiadeans, and 110–115 of dactylic hexameters.

(b) In order to understand Seneca's use of mixed rhythm, a few words ought to be said about the ways in which he imitated the meters of Horace. In addition to direct borrowing of, e.g., asclepiadeans, glyconics etc., and to composing, for example, the Sapphic strophe in such a way that more than three sapphic lines could precede the adonic, he also used Horatian meters in an abbreviated or altered form.

For example, *Oedipus* 405: $\overset{-\,\smile\,-}{lucidum}\ \overset{-\,-\,\smile\,\smile}{caeli\ decus,}\ \overset{-\,\smile-//}{huc\ ades}$ is a sapphic minus its last syllable, i.e. cr ˄gl// instead of cr ˄hipp//;

in *Agamemno* 812: $\overset{-\,\smile}{impar(em)}\ \overset{-\,-\,-\,\smile\smile\,-\,-//}{aequasti:\ tuus\ ille}$ the last two syllables have been clipped off the sapphic (= cr ˄ph//). A similar playfulness is displayed with other meters.

As an example of mixed rhythm, we shall examine *Oedipus* 403–411:

$$\overline{}\overline{}\ -\ \cup\cup-\cup\ \cup\ -\ /--\ \cup\ \cup-\ -\ //$$
effusam redimite comam nutante corymbo,   6 da$_\wedge$ //

$$-\cup\cup\ -\ --/-\ -\ -\ -\ \cup\cup\ \ --\ //$$
mollia Nysaeis armati bracchia thyrsis!   6 da$_\wedge$ //

405
$$-\cup-\ \ --\ \cup\cup\ \ -\ \cup-\ //$$
lucidum caeli decus, huc ades   cr $_\wedge$gl//

$$-\ -\ \ -\ \cup\cup\ -\cup-//$$
votis quae tibi nobiles   gl//

$$-\ \ -\ \ -\ \ \cup\ \ \cup-/$$
Thebae, Bacche, tuae   ph$_\wedge$ /
(= hem/)

$$-\ \ -\ \ -\ \ \cup\cup\ -\ \cup\ -\ //$$
palmis supplicibus ferunt.   gl//

$$-\ \ -\ \ -\cup\ \cup\ -\ /\ -\ \cup\cup-\ \ \cup-/$$
huc adverte favens virgineum caput,   gl^c/

410
$$-\ \ -\ -\cup\cup-/-\ \cup\cup\ -\cup-\ //$$
vultu sidereo discute nubila   gl^c//

$$-\ \ -\ -\ \cup\ \cup-\ \ \cup\ -\ \cup\cup\ -\ \ \cup\ --\ //$$
et tristes Erebi minas avidumque fatum.
hem (= ph$_\wedge$)$_\wedge$hipp//

The sequence starts out with two introductory dactylic hexameters, but thereafter a glyconic pattern predominates: line 405 is a catalectic sapphic, i.e., a cretic + an acephalous glyconic, then follows a glyconic, and then an asclepiadean taken to its caesura which might also be interpreted as a dactylic hemiepes. After a further glyconic, there are two asclepiadeans, and the clausula of the whole piece combines the dactylic movement of the beginning with the Aeolics of the rest.

XX. Later Developments

Two factors influenced the development of post-classical verse. In the first place, the meters used by the classical poets, especially Vergil and Horace, remained a living force in the tradition, despite the rise of Christianity. Correct verse in Vergilian and Horatian style was written by Nemesianus, Ausonius, Claudian, Rutilius Namatianus, to mention but a few. Christian poets such as Prudentius, Boethius and others also wrote in the classical forms. At the same time, there was a tendency towards the trivial and the bizarre, which took the form of centos made up of Vergilian tags (e.g., the *Cento Nuptialis* of Ausonius), of poems written in the shape of the object described (e.g., an axe, an altar, etc.), of acrostics, and of poems written in monosyllables. There also developed the use of Greek lyric forms (taken mainly from Horace) in ways not used before, e.g., the stichic use of meters such as the clausula of the Sapphic strophe. Many of these types have been mentioned above in the various sections on the lyric meters.

In the Church service, hymns which were meant to be sung assumed a special place. The earliest writer of Latin hymns was Hilary of Poitiers (d. A.D. 367), who, in his travels in the East from A.D. 350 to 360, was inspired with the idea of writing a book of Latin hymns. Fragments of three of his hymns were discovered at Arezzo late in the nineteenth century. Although Hilary, like many late Latin authors, takes liberties with the quantity of syllables (e.g. the final syllable of *pater* in the last line of the passage quoted below), the classical structure of his hymns made them unpopular and probably difficult to sing. In the first of these hymns, the stanzas are arranged in alphabetical sequence, the first beginning with *A*, the second with *B*, and so on. Each period consists of a glyconic followed by an asclepiadean or by an alcaic hendecasyllable. E.g., Bulst I 1, Strophe A:

Ante saecula qui manens — gl/

semperque nate, semper ut est pater, — ia ₐgl//

namque te sine quomodo — gl/

dici, ni pater est, quod pater sit, potest? glᶜ///

The true father of Latin hymnody was St Ambrose (bishop of Milan A.D. 374–397). Some four of the extant Ambrosian hymns are definitely attributed to him. All are written in iambic dimeters and follow the Greek practice which does not allow substitutions in the even feet, a practice neglected by Plautus and Terence. Of equal interest is the use of stichic sequences in stanza form. Each hymn consists of 32 lines arranged in eight four-line stanzas, a form especially useful for alternate choirs singing the same melody. Further evidence for the importance of music is that, while a longum may replace a breve in the odd feet, there are few resolutions. This would indicate that one syllable was to be sung to one note. It is even possible that the same melody was used for all hymns. The ease of teaching this kind of hymn to a congregation must in part account for their popularity and the continual imitation which later occurred. The list of so-called "ambrosian" hymns is quite extensive. Here are the first two stanzas of Ambrose's hymn "Ad Horam Incensi" which are quoted by St Augustine, *Confessions* IX. 12. 32 (Bulst II 4):

Deus creator omnium	2 ia//
polique rector, vestiens	2 ia//
diem decoro lumine,	2 ia//
noctem soporis gratia,	2 ia///
artus solutos ut quies	2 ia//
reddat laboris usui	2 ia//
mentesque fessas allevet	2 ia//
luctusque solvat anxios,	2 ia///

The simple meter, the coincidence of syntactical structure and metric structure, the end-stopped lines and stanzas, and the parallelism of the two-stanza groups, all are characteristic not only of the hymn, but of much medieval verse in general.

More important in the long run was the second factor influencing the development of post-classical verse. By the fourth century A.D., Latin vowels had begun to lose their quantitative differences while retaining their qualitative differences. Stress accent began to affect vowel quantity, as it had already done at an earlier period in iambic shortening (cf. above, section II. 4). Thus, a vowel in a stressed syllable tended to be lengthened, and at the same time a long vowel in an unstressed position might be shortened. At about the same time, an interest in rhyme, best defined as the assonance of the last two syllables of two consecutive lines, became more marked. The origin and development of rhythmic and rhymed Latin verse is a matter of great controversy and lies beyond the scope and intention of this handbook. Undoubtedly, the weakening of the sensitivity to quantity, the increased use of music (especially in the Christian congregations), and the parallel development of rhythmical prose, all contributed to these changes in poetic technique.*

These tendencies are best exemplified in the development of the Christian Latin hymn. The earliest extant example of a hymn written in rhythmical Latin poetry, St Augustine's *Psalm against the Donatists*, beset though it is with textual difficulties,† is most instructive in this respect. Of this poem Augustine himself says: "*non aliquo carminis genere id fieri volui,*

---

* For a complete discussion of medieval Latin versification, see Dag Norberg, *Introduction à l'étude de la versification latine médiévale, Studia Latina Stockholmiensia* 5 (Stockholm 1958).

† The best text is that of C. Lambot in *Revue Bénédictine* 47 (1935) 312–330, also to be found in Bulst, pp. 139–146.

ne me necessitas metrica ad aliqua verba, quae vulgo minus sunt usitata, compelleret." (*Retractationes* I. 20).

This poem contains, in addition to a one-line refrain, a prologue of five verses, 20 strophes of a dozen verses each, which begin with one of the letters of the alphabet (i.e., *A–V* of the Latin alphabet), and an epilogue of 30 verses. The prologue, the strophes, and the epilogue were recited to the congregation which answered with the refrain, or *hypopsalma* as it is called. All the lines consist of 16 syllables (elision and synizesis can occur but are not always demanded), divided by a diaeresis after the eighth syllable. Hiatus is permitted only at the central diaeresis, and of course at the end of the line. The refrain consists of 17 syllables. Here is the refrain and the first four verses of *A*:

Omnes qui gaudetis de páce, modo verum iudicáte.

Abundantia peccatórum solet fratres conturbáre.

propter hoc dominus nóster voluit nos praemonére,

comparans regnum caelórum reticulo miss(o) in máre:

congregavit multos písces omne genus hinc et índe. . . .

Certain facts of the rhythmical structure are clear: the alphabetical arrangement, the equal number of syllables in each line, the regularity of the medial diaeresis, the penultimate accent of the word at the diaeresis and of the word at the end of the line (exceptions: *accípere* in line 2 and *hómine* in line 31), and the final assonance, or rhyme, in *-e*. No satisfactory answer has yet been given to the question on what classical quantitative meter, if any, Augustine modelled this poem, but the scarcity of available material (the *Psalm* is an isolated example of its type and period) must make any solution tentative at the present state of our knowledge. An attractive

118

view, but one open to very many objections, is that Augustine had in mind the trochaic octonarius of dramatic verse (see above, section VIII. 2). Since we have no idea how the trochaic octonarius was read in the fourth century A.D., no definite decision can be reached. It is also possible that Augustine borrowed the form of this poem from psalms chanted by his Donatist adversaries. Here again the lack of literary evidence for these psalms leaves us still in the dark.

Yet the importance of this poem can hardly be over-estimated. Medieval Latin rhythmical poetry is character-ized by certain traits already apparent in the *Psalm*: absence of a strict quantitative structure, isosyllabic lines, accentual cadence, and frequent use of rhyme.

Classical Latin meters continued, however, to be written and had a long and distinguished history throughout the Middle Ages. Further, it may be noted that one of the finest post-classical Latin poets was none other than John Milton, whose collection of Latin verse was published at London in 1645.

Glossary of Technical Terms

acatalectic: = "not coming to an abrupt end". The opposite of "catalectic", see under *catalexis*. A verse is called *acatalectic* when no element is suppressed before the pause.

acephaly: = "headlessness". The lack of one element at the beginning of a (usually Aeolic) meter. See sections 1, 16, and I.

Aeolic meters: The meters first found in lyric poetry written in the Aeolic dialect, especially by Sappho and Alcaeus. See sections 16, 17. 4, and XVI.

Alcaic stanza: A strophe consisting of two alcaic hendecasyllables, an alcaic enneasyllable, and an alcaic decasyllable. See section XVIII near end.

anaclasis: = "bending back". The process whereby a short element changes its place with an adjacent long element, e.g., ∪∪–– becomes ∪–∪–. See sections 13 and XIII. 2 (b).

anacrusis: = "upbeat". A term, adopted in a technical sense only in modern times to describe one or more syllables at the beginning of a period which remain outside the limits of the meter.

anceps: more fully: *elementum anceps* = "two-headed element". Space for either one short or one long syllable in a metrical unit; e.g., the first element of an iambic metron is anceps, and the "base" of Aeolic meters consists of two ancipitia. See sections 1 and I.

antistrophe: = "counterturn" in dancing. A metrical system in Greek choral lyric consisting of a given number of periods, which repeat the metrical structure of the strophe preceding it. See also under *strophe, responsion,* and sections 17 and 18.

aphaeresis: = "taking away". The converse of *elision,* i.e., the suppression in hiatus of the short initial vowel of the second word, e.g., ἀγαθή 'στιν, *dictum (e)st.* See sections 3 note and II. 2.

apocope: = "cutting off". The suppression of a final vowel before a consonant, e.g., ἀναβαίνω becomes ἀμβαίνω.

arsis and thesis: These terms refer originally to the "raising" and "lowering" respectively of the foot in Greek dancing and beating rhythm. Late Roman metricians transferred the terms to the raising and lowering of the voice. Scholars in the eighteenth and nineteenth centuries called *arsis* that part of a metron or foot which is normally occupied by long elements and *thesis* the part normally occupied by short elements. Thus, a dactyl was described as a "falling" rhythm, because in it the arsis precedes the thesis. Because of the confusion inherent in this variety of usage, and in order to prevent false analogies with the "beat" in modern music, modern metrics tries to avoid these terms.

asynarteton: = "not joined together". A verse consisting of two or more metrical units which follow one another without pause, but are separated by diaeresis. See sections 15. 2 and XV. 2.

blunt: A period is called *blunt* when its last metron is incomplete and the final longum is preceded by a breve. See section 10. 3.

break: Place within a meter where word ending is demanded or recommended; generic term for caesura and diaeresis. See sections 4 and IV.

brevis brevians: See under *iambic shortening.*

brevis in longo: more fully: *syllaba brevis in elemento longo.* A short syllable occupying the invariably long last element of a period. See sections 3. 3 and III. 3.

bridge: Place within a meter where word ending is forbidden or avoided. See sections 4 and IV.

bucolic diaeresis: In the dactylic hexameter, diaeresis after a trisyllabic fourth metron. See sections 5 and V.

caesura: Break within a metron where word ending is demanded or recommended. See sections 4 and IV.

canticum: In the strict sense, a recitative portion of Roman drama, probably declaimed to the accompaniment of a flute. The term is also used as a short form of *mutatis modis canticum* (q.v.). See sections VII, IX, and XIX.

catalexis: = "coming to an abrupt end". The suppression of the final element of a meter before a pause. See sections 1, 3. 4, I and III. 4.

clausula: A metrical unit which rounds off and "closes" an asynarteton or a longer series. E.g., the ithyphallic is the clausula of the archilochean period; the paroemiac often closes a series of anapaestic dimeters.

colon: = "limb." A unit of verse in lyric poetry. Usually several cola are thought to make up a period.

compounding: The external or internal extension of an Aeolic meter. See sections 16 and XVI. 2.

correption: = "seizing". The shortening of a long final vowel (or diphthong) before a word beginning with a vowel (or diphthong). See section 5 near end.

Dactylo-epitrite: A type of meter used in Greek choral lyric. So called because it is sometimes regarded as consisting of dactyls and epitrites ($--\cup-$). See section 17. 2.

diaeresis: = "taking apart". Place between two metra (or feet) where word ending is demanded or recommended. See sections 4 and IV.

digamma: The Greek letter F (pronounced like *w*) which disappeared from many Greek dialects at an early stage, but which exercises an influence on, e.g., the Homeric hexameter by closing seemingly open syllables and by seemingly permitting hiatus.

dimeter: Metrical unit consisting of two metra.

dipody: = "two-footer". A term sometimes used in Latin spoken verse to describe a phrase consisting of two feet (usually = one metron).

distich: = "two-liner". A unit consisting of two unlike periods, e.g., the elegiac couplet (see sections 6 and VI) which consists of 6 da$_\wedge$// + 2 hemiepes//.

diverbium: The spoken portion of Roman drama. See section VII.

Dorian: An older name for *Dactylo-epitrite.*

elegiac: Verse composed in distichs, each consisting of 6 da$_\wedge$// + 2 hemiepes//. See sections 6 and VI.

element: The space occupied by a longum, by a breve, or by an anceps in conformity with the basic structure of a given metrical scheme.

elision: The suppression of a final vowel (in Latin also of a final vowel + -*m*) before an initial vowel (in Latin also initial *h*-) in the following word. Indicated in Greek by an apostrophe; e.g., πολλ᾽ ἔστιν, *Troian(o) a sanguine*. See sections 3 note, and II. 2.

enjambement: The run-over of a word, of a grammatical unit, or of a unit of thought from one period to the next.

epigram: A short, pointed poem consisting of one or more elegiac distichs. See sections 6 and VI.

epode: = "after-song". (*a*) A metrical system in Greek choral lyric which follows and rounds off strophe and antistrophe. It is usually composed in a metrical structure different from that of strophe-antistrophe. See sections 17 and 18.

(*b*) A distich or couplet of lyric, composed of two different periods which may or may not be based upon the same meter. See sections 15. 1 and XV. 1.

foot: The smallest metrical unit of Latin spoken verse, consisting of a given sequence and number of short and long syllables; e.g., an iambic foot (∪—) consists of one short and long element. Usually two feet (= dipody) are equivalent to one metron. See sections V and VII.

hephthemimeral caesura: In dactylic hexameters, the caesura after the fourth longum.

hexameter, dactylic: A spoken verse, consisting of six dactylic metra (= six dactylic feet in Latin), the last of which is dissyllabic. See sections 5 and V.

hiatus: The "gap" between a word ending in a vowel (or diphthong) and a word beginning with a vowel (or diphthong). See sections 3. 2, II. 2, and III. 2.

hypermetric verse: A verse exhibiting a metrical continuity from one line to the next, usually brought about by the elision of a final vowel at the end of a line before the opening vowel of the following line. The term is also used to describe a meter which exceeds the usual length by one longum. See also under *synapheia*.

iambic shortening: = *brevis brevians*. A rule governing iambs, trochees, and some other meters in Roman drama. According to this rule, a long syllable, if preceded by a short syllable, may be counted as short, if the natural word accent falls on the syllable immediately preceding or following it. See section II. 4.

ictus: = "stress", "beat". An emphasis in pronunciation which, as some modern metricians believe, is to be placed upon the arsis (or on the first syllable of the arsis) of every metron or foot; e.g., in a dactyl the ictus is regarded as falling upon the first syllable, and in an iamb upon the second syllable. Whether Greek and Latin poetry actually had ictus or not is still controversial.

Ionic meters: The generic term which covers ionics, anaclasts, and choriambs. See sections 13 and XIII.

logaoedic: = "spoken–sung". A term, no longer used, which refers to verses mixed of iambs, dactyls, trochees, and anapaests.

Meineke's Law: The discovery by the German scholar August Meineke that the number of periods in each of Horace's odes is divisible by four. See section XVIII.

mesode: = "mid-song". A short astrophic system in Greek dramatic lyric which is occasionally sandwiched between strophe and antistrophe. See section 18.

meter: The rhythmical pattern in which a period of poetry (other than an asynarteton) is composed.

metron: = "measure". The smallest metrical unit, consisting of a given sequence and number of long and short elements, of a period made up of several such units. E.g., an iambic metron ($\times - \cup -$) repeated three times constitutes the period called "iambic trimeter". In Latin spoken verse the foot rather than the metron is the minimal unit.

monody: A sung lyric solo.

mora: = "delay". The smallest musical or rhythmical element; it is the length of time required for the enunciation of one short syllable.

mutatis modis canticum: The sung portion of Roman drama; sometimes called simply *canticum*. See sections VII, IX, and XIX.

octonarius, iambic or *trochaic:* A Latin meter consisting of eight complete feet, corresponding to the Greek acatalectic tetrameter. See sections VII. 3 and VIII. 2.

pause: An emphatic break in a metrical scheme that separates one period from another. See sections 3 and III.

pendant: A period is called *pendant* when its last metron is incomplete and the final longum is preceded by a longum. See section 10. 3.

penthemimeral caesura: In dactylic hexameters, the caesura after the third longum.

Penultimate Law: The rule governing the natural word accent of Latin: if the penultimate (= next-to-last) syllable of a word is long, it receives the word accent; if it is short, the word accent falls on the syllable preceding it. See *Introduction* to *Latin Meters*.

period: (*a*) A "line" of poetry marked off from the next by means of a pause. See sections 3 and III.

(*b*) The term is also used (but not in this book) to describe a group of periods rounded off by a clausula within a stanza, and

(*c*) the structure of a whole stanza.

Porson's Law: The discovery by the British scholar Richard Porson that in Greek tragic trimeters the anceps of the third metron cannot be occupied by a long syllable terminating a word. See section 4.

positio debilis: The position of a short vowel before a combination of mute + liquid (or nasal) consonants.

proode: = "fore-song". A short astrophic system in Greek dramatic lyric, found occasionally before a strophe. See section 18.

resolution: The substitution of two short syllables for one longum, one anceps, or one breve.

responsion: The parallelism of metric schemes between strophe and strophe or strophe and antistrophe. See sections 10. 3(c) note and 18.

rhyme: The connection of two periods by means of assonance of the last word(s) in each period ("end rhyme"). Also found within a period by assonance of the last word(s) before the break with the last word(s) before the pause ("internal rhyme"). See sections V near end and XX.

rhythm: = "flow". The patterned movement of verse brought about, in Greek and Latin, by a regular or recognizable sequence of long and short elements.

Sapphic stanza: A strophe consisting of three sapphic hendecasyllables, the last with the final long element missing, and an acephalous pherecratean. See section XVIII.

Saturnian: The oldest and only extant indigenous Latin meter. The problem whether its rhythm is accentual or quantitative is still unsolved. See *Note* at the end of *Introduction* to *Latin Meters.*

senarius, iambic: A Latin meter consisting of six iambic feet, corresponding to the Greek iambic trimeter. *Senarii,* without a qualifying adjective, refers to the spoken portions of Roman drama. See section VII. 1.

septenarius, iambic or *trochaic:* A Latin meter consisting of seven feet + one additional syllable, corresponding to the Greek catalectic tetrameter. See sections VII. 2 and VIII 1.

stichic composition: Composition "by line", in which one and the same period is repeated throughout the whole poem. E.g., an epic poem is a stichic composition in dactylic hexameters. See sections 9, 20. 1, IX near end, and XVII.

strophe: = a "turn" in dancing. A metrical system in Greek lyric, consisting of a number of periods which may or may not be identical in length and in meter. In choral poetry the strophe is followed by an antistrophe consisting of the same number of periods of the same length and in the same sequence of meters. The term *strophe* is sometimes also used interchangeably with *stanza.* See also under *antistrophe, reponsion,* and sections 17 and 18.

synaloephe: = "smearing together". The treatment as one of two separate vowels, one at the end of a word and the other at the beginning of the next word. See section 2.

synapheia: = "fastening together". The combination of two lines of verse into one period by avoiding a pause between them. E.g., in iambic trimeters two lines are said to be in *synapheia* if the first is hypermetric.

syncope: = "beating together". The suppression of a short vowel between two consonants within a word, e.g., *pueritia* becomes *puertia.*

synizesis: = "settling together". The treatment as one of two adjoining vowels within the same word. See sections 2 and II. 3.

tetrameter, trochaic: A catalectic verse consisting of three complete and one catalectic trochaic metra. See sections 8 and XII. 2.

thesis: See *arsis and thesis.*

trimeter, iambic: An acatalectic verse consisting of three iambic metra. See sections 7 and XII. 1.

versus quadratus: A form of the trochaic septenarius used in popular verses. See section VIII. 1.

vocalis ante vocalem corripitur: A rule according to which a syllable ending in a long vowel is shortened, if the syllable is followed by another vowel; e.g., *flĕo,* but *flēre.* There are, however, many exceptions to this rule. See also *correption.*

zeugma: = *bridge* (q.v.).

List of Meters

		See section
adonic	— ∪ ∪ — —	xv. 2 near end and xviii
alcaic decasyllable	— ∪ ∪ — ∪ ∪ — ∪ — —	xviii near end
alcaic enneasyllable	× — ∪ — × — ∪ — —	xviii near end
alcaic hendecasyllable	× — ∪ — × — ∪ ∪ — ∪ —	xvi. 2 (b) and xviii near end
amphibrach	∪ — ∪	
anaclast	∪ ∪ — ∪ — ∪ — —	13 and xiii. 2 (b)
anacreontic = anaclast		
anapaest	∪∪ ∪∪ ∪∪	11 and xi
antispast	∪ — — ∪	
archebulean	× — ∪ ∪ — ∪ ∪ — ∪ ∪ —	
archilochean:		
(a) enopl/ith//	× — ∪ ∪ — ∪ ∪ — /— ∪ — —	15. 2
(b) 4 da∪∪/ith//	— ∪ ∪ — ∪ ∪ — ∪ ∪ — ∪ ∪/— ∪ — —	15. 3, xii. 4, and xv. 2 and 3
aristophanean	— ∪ ∪ — ∪ — —	xvi. 2 (b) and xviii
asclepiadean gl^c//	× × — ∪ ∪ — — ∪ ∪ — ∪ —	16 and xvi. 2 (a)
asclepiadean, major gl^{2c}//	× × — ∪ ∪ — — ∪ ∪ — — ∪ ∪ — ∪ —	16 and xvi. 2 (a)

		See section
bacchiac	∪ — —	12 and XII. 3
choliamb	× — ∪ — × — ∪ — — —	7 and XII. 1
choriamb	— ∪ ∪ —	13 and XIII. 1
cretic	— ∪ —	12 and XII. 3
dactyl	— ∪͞∪	5, 6, 10, V, VI, and X
diphilean = choerilean	— ∪∪ — ∪∪ — × — ∪∪ — ∪∪ —	XV. 2
dochmiac	× — — ∪ —	19
elegiambic	— ∪∪ — ∪∪ —/× — ∪ — × — ∪ —	XV. 2 and 3
encomiologicus	— ∪∪ — ∪∪ —/×⫶— ∪ — —	15 and 17. 2
enoplion	× — ∪͞∪ — ∪∪ —	15 and XV. 2 note
eupolidean		
polysch/polysch∧//	with many resolutions	13 and XIII. 2 (b) near end
galliambic 4 io∧// or anacl/2 io∧//		16 and XVI
glyconic	× × — ∪∪ — ∪ —	
hemiambic	× — ∪ — ∪ — —	6, VI, and X
hemiepes	— ∪∪ — ∪∪ —	16 and XVI
hipponactean	× × — ∪∪ — ∪ — —	
hypodochmiac	— ∪ — ∪ —	
iamb	× — ∪ — (or foot: ∪ —)	7, 12, VII, and XII. 1

		See section
iambelegiac (a)	× — ∪ — / — ∪ ∪ — ∪ ∪ —	xv. 2 and 3
(b)	× — ∪ — × — ∪ — / — ∪ ∪ — ∪ ∪	
ibycean	— ∪ ∪ — ∪ ∪ — ∪ —	
ionic a maiore	— — ∪ ∪	13 and xiii. 2
ionic a minore	∪ ∪ — —	12 and xii. 4
ithyphallic	— ∪ — ∪ — —	12 and xii. 4
lecythion	— ∪ — × — ∪ —	12 note and xii note
molossus	— — —	12 note and xii note
paeon, first	— ∪ ∪ ∪	
fourth	∪ ∪ ∪ —	
palimbacchiac	— — ∪	
paroemiac 2 an∧//	⏓⏓ — ⏓⏓ — / — ∪ ∪ — —	11 and xi
pentameter	— ⏓⏓ — ⏓⏓ — / — ∪ ∪ — ∪ ∪ —	6 and vi
penthemimer	× — ∪ — —	xviii near end
phalaecean hendecasyllable	× × — ∪ ∪ — ∪ — ∪ — —	xii. 4 and xvi. 2 (b)
gl ba//		
pherecratean	× × — ∪ ∪ — —	16 and xvi
polyschematist	× × — × — ∪ ∪ —	
praxilleion	— ∪ ∪ — ∪ ∪ — —	
priapean gl/ph//	× × — ∪ ∪ — ∪ — / × × — ∪ ∪ — ∪ — —	13 and xiii. 1 (b)
proceleusmatic	∪ ∪ ∪ ∪	16 and xv. 2

131

		See section
prosodiac	× – ⏑ ⏑ – ⏑ ⏑ –	xv. 2 note
pyrrhic	⏑ ⏑	
reizianum	× – ⏑ ⏑ – –	16 and xvi near end
sapphic enneasyllable = hipponactean	– ⏑ × – ⏑ ⏑ – ⏑ –	16, xvi. 2 (b), and xviii
sapphic hendecasyllable cr‿hipp//	– ⏑ × – ⏑ ⏑ – ⏑ – –	
sapphic 14-syllable gl²ᵈ//	× × – ⏑ ⏑ – ⏑ ⏑ – ⏑ –	xvi. 2 (b)
sapphic, major cr‿hippᶜ//	– ⏑ × – ⏑ ⏑ – ⏑ ⏑ – ⏑ –	
simmiacus 5 da‿//	⏑ ⏑ – ⏑ ⏑ – ⏑ ⏑ – ⏑ ⏑ –	
scazon = choliamb		
sotadean	– ⏑ ⏑ – ⏑ – ⏑ – ⏑ –	xiii. 2 (b)
spondee	– –	vi
stesichorean	– ⏑ × – ⏑ – × – ⏑ – (–)	
telesilleion	× – ⏑ ⏑ – ⏑ –	16
tribrach	⏑ ⏑ ⏑	
trochee	– ⏑ × (or foot: – ⏑)	8, 12, viii, and xii. 2

Index of Greek Authors Cited

Index of Latin Authors Cited